Y0-BOH-473

SCHOOLS IN TRANSITION:
THE PRACTITIONER AS CHANGE AGENT

|I|D|E|A| REPORTS ON SCHOOLING
JOHN I. GOODLAD, *General Editor and Director*

EARLY SCHOOLING SERIES
Assisted by Jerrold M. Novotney

SERIES ON EDUCATIONAL CHANGE
Assisted by Kenneth A. Tye

LA
217
T93

SCHOOLS IN TRANSITION:
The Practitioner As Change Agent

Kenneth A. Tye and
Jerrold M. Novotney

Foreword by
Samuel G. Sava
Executive Director |I|D|E|A|

Introduction by
John I. Goodlad

A CHARLES F. KETTERING FOUNDATION PROGRAM

McGRAW-HILL BOOK COMPANY
New York   St. Louis   San Francisco   Düsseldorf
London   Mexico   Sydney   Toronto

WITHDRAWN
WEBERT LIBRARY
Pacific College - M. B. Seminary
Fresno, Calif. 93702

42862

Copyright © 1975 by the Institute for Development of Educational Activities, Inc. All rights reserved. Printed in the United States of America. No part of this publication may be reproduced, stored in a retrieval system, or transmitted, in any form or by any means, electronic, mechanical, photocopying, recording, or otherwise, without the prior written permission of the publisher.

Library of Congress Cataloging in Publication Data

Tye, Kenneth A.
  Schools in transition.

IDEA(Series on educational change)
    "A Charles F. Kettering Foundation Program "
    Bibliography: p.
    Includes index.
    1. Education—United States. I. Novotney, Jerrold M. joint author. II. Title.
III. Series: Institute for Development of Educational Activities. Series on educational change.

LA217.T93   370'973   75-15843
ISBN 0-07-065690-8

|I|D|E|A| is the service mark for the Institute for Development of Educational Activities, Inc., an incorporated affiliate of the Charles F. Kettering Foundation.

|I|D|E|A| was established in 1965 to encourage constructive change in elementary and secondary schools. It serves as the primary operant for the Foundation's missions and programs in education.

As an institution committed to stimulating constructive changes for the benefit of mankind, the Kettering Foundation believes strongly in the potential of education to help bring about such changes.

Robert G. Chollar

President and
Chief Executive Officer
Charles F. Kettering Foundation

Acknowledgments for permission to use excerpts from copyrighted material include:

Eugene L. Belisle and Cyril G. Sargent, "The Concept of Administration." Copyright 1957 by Eugene L. Belisle and Cyril G. Sargent. Used by permission of Harper & Row, Publishers, Inc.

Mary F. Bentzen and Kenneth A. Tye, "Change in Elementary Schools." Copyright 1973 by Mary M. Bentzen and Kenneth A. Tye. Used by permission of the National Society for the Study of Education.

Roald F. Campbell and Donald H. Layton, *Policy Making for American Education.* Copyright 1969 by Roald F. Campbell and Donald H. Layton. Used by permission of Roald F. Campbell and Administrator's Notebook.

Terry D. Cornell, *Performances and Process Objectives.* Copyright 1970 by Terry D. Cornell. Used by permission of Phi Delta Kappan.

Lawrence W. Downey, "Organizational Theory as a Guide to Educational Change." Copyright January 1961 by Lawrence W. Downey. Used by permission of Educational Theory.

Lawrence W. Downey, "Direction Amid Change." Copyright February 1961 by Lawrence W. Downey. Used by permission of Phi Delta Kappan.

Mario Fantini, "Alternatives within Public Schools." Copyright March 1973 by Mario Fantini. Used by permission of Phi Delta Kappan.

Max L. Feldman, "Transportation: An Equal Opportunity for Access." Copyright 1968 by Max L. Feldman. Used by permission of Indiana University Press.

John I. Goodlad et al., *Early Schooling in the United States.* Copyright 1973 by the Institute for Development of Educational Activities, Inc. Used by permission of the Institute.

John I. Goodlad et al., *Toward a Mankind School: An Adventure in Humanistic Education.* Copyright 1974 by Educational Inquiry, Inc. Used by permission of Educational Inquiry, Inc.

J. W. Getzels, "Conflict and Role Behavior in the Educational Setting." Copyright 1963 by Allyn and Bacon, Inc. Used by permission of Allyn and Bacon, Inc.

Warren T. Greenleaf and Gary A. Griffin, *Schools for the Seventies and Beyond: A Call to Action.* Copyright 1971 by Warren T. Greenleaf and Gary A. Griffin. Used by permission of the National Education Association.

Morris Janowitz, *Institution Building in Urban Education.* Copyright 1969 by Russell Sage Foundation. Used by permission of the Foundation.

Bruce Joyce and Marsha Weil, *Models of Teaching.* Copyright 1972 by Bruce Joyce and Marsha Weil. Used by permission of Prentice-Hall, Inc.

Donald N. Michael, *The Unprepared Society: Planning for a Precarious Future.* Copyright 1968 by Donald N. Michael. Used by permission of Basic Books, Inc., Publishers.

North Carolina Department of Public Instruction, *Accountability: Review of Literature and Recommendations for Implementation.* Copyright May 1972 by the State Department of Public Instruction. Used by permission of the Department.

Jerrold M. Novotney and Kenneth A. Tye, *The Dynamics of Educational Leadership.* Copyright 1973 by Jerrold M. Novotney and Kenneth A. Tye. Used by permission of Educational Resource Associates, Inc.

Ole Sand, "Strategies for Change." Copyright 1971 by Ole Sand. Used by permission of the National Society for the Study of Education.

Vernon H. Smith, "Options in Public Education: The Quiet Revolution." Copyright March 1973 by Vernon H. Smith. Used by permission of Phi Delta Kappan.

Bernard C. Watson, "Rebuilding the System: Practical Goal or Impossible Dream?" Copyright February 1971 by Bernard C. Watson. Used by permission of Phi Delta Kappan.

CONTENTS

FOREWORD

The authors of this volume participated in the Study of Educational Change and School Improvement conducted by the Research Division of the Institute for Development of Educational Activities, Inc. (|I|D|E|A|), under the direction of John I. Goodlad. They worked with schools that were trying to change and improve themselves. They observed the conditions that constrained the schools' efforts and ideas and techniques which seemed to promote progress. These observations pointed to the need for and formed the basis of this book.

|I|D|E|A| was established by the Charles F. Kettering Foundation in 1965 as its educational affiliate and given the specific mission of accelerating the pace of change in education. Rather than advocate yet another collection of "innovations" based on the best insights then available, we decided to begin by examining the total context in which change was to take place. In the *Study of Educational Change and School Improvement,* eighteen schools from eighteen southern California districts were selected to form the League of Cooperating Schools and to participate in the design and testing of a new strategy for educational improvement. Other volumes in the |I|D|E|A| REPORTS series describe the strategy and the results of the study.

In view of continuing public criticism of the schools, our apparent inability to rescue many of our children from academic mediocrity or failure, and the widely felt need for more tested-and-proven innovations, the Study of Change may be one of the most important studies of education ever undertaken. But pedagogical literature is littered with the corpses of past studies, many of them excellent, that failed to affect educational practice. Will this study make any difference?

We believe so. In addition to issuing results of the study, |I|D|E|A| has incorporated this change strategy into a school improvement program aimed at individualizing education, a new model of school organization necessary to permit the accommodation of individual differences, and an intensive, clinical training component for teachers and administrators. We call this the |I|D|E|A| Change Program for Individually Guided Education (IGE).

As this volume goes to press, more than 1,000 elementary and secondary schools in thirty-five states have adopted the IGE program, and the program has spread to American-sponsored schools in approximately two dozen other countries. It is clear that IGE, together with the research and development work on which it rests, already has had an influence on American education.

On behalf of |I|D|E|A| and the Charles F. Kettering Foundation, I wish to express gratitude to the school board officials, administrators, teachers, and parents whose cooperation made the Study of Change possible. They have advanced the day when change will become a way of life in education, rather than a sporadic, temporary, and usually disappointing confrontation with forces that we have not previously understood.

Samuel G. Sava
Executive Director
|I|D|E|A|

INTRODUCTION

Many thoughtful analysts of the national and world scene are deeply concerned about the apparent erosion of our most fundamental institutions. They cite corruption in high places, political interference in the operation of the courts, the sacrifice of the people's welfare in the pursuit of self-interests, reinterpretation of the concept of community to reflect segmented or parochial concerns, indecisiveness and drift on the part of our designated leaders. And they point to accompanying cynicism on the part of the citizenry.

When confidence in ourselves and our institutions is at a low ebb, the institution almost always singled out for special condemnation is the school. Perhaps this is because we have had too much faith in it; perhaps it is because most of us have been through it, think we know something about it, and are sure we know what to do about it; perhaps it is because it can be reduced to specific places and people, becoming less faceless than the unseen "they" who somewhere run everything so badly. At any rate, in recent years confidence in the schools reached a new low and the extremes of what to do a new high:

> In the last few years a flood of books has appeared purporting to show that public education in the United States is a delusion and a fraud, that it is not merely defective, it is positively damaging to the children who have to submit to it. The more extreme critics propose, therefore, not to reform public education, but to abolish it.*

There is no doubt that the breadth and depth of attacks on and disillusionment with the schools have seriously damaged the sense of worth and potency of those who work in them. We know that prolonged lack of faith in individuals frequently becomes a self-fulfilling prophecy. Why should it not become so for institutions as well?

In 1966, I brought together a group of men and women to test a converse proposition: that given support and encouragement, those working in schools would develop feelings of self-worth, a sense of personal and collective power, and a higher level of professional behavior and that these qualities in turn would produce a greater readiness for and performance of constructive changes or reforms. An implied assumption was that there is no point in endeavoring to improve children's reading scores or any other of their academic behaviors with

---

* Robert M. Hutchins, "Two Fateful Decisions," *The Center Magazine*, vol. 8, no. 1, January/February 1975, p. 7.

new methods that are used half-heartedly by demoralized teachers. In effect, the needed reconstruction of schooling must begin with the adults in the school and the social systems they constitute, not with pedagogy, materials, and pupil achievement.

This may appear to be a most benign proposition in our era of "get-well-quick" panaceas crying for public attention. And it certainly is not a proposition destined to get much attention from a news-oriented press. As one young reporter snorted when I tried to explain, "Don't give me your graduate seminar, just the headings and subheadings." No, it is not an eye-catching or mind-boggling proposition but careful examination reveals it to be a potentially powerful countervailing one.

In large part because of general failure to understand what Seymour Sarason has termed "the culture of the school" and to take that culture into account in seeking to change schooling practices, reformers usually have viewed the pupils as the target, referring to them collectively as products. In their most extreme form, resulting approaches have tended to do end runs around teachers by means of performance contracts and "teacher-proof" materials. Such approaches have tended to alienate rather than to engage the interest and support of teachers. Failure almost inevitably has been the result.

What we had in mind did not exclude outside forces for change. But it placed the emphasis on preparing the ground, readying those within the schools for constructive change by first developing both individual and group propensity for self-improvement. We worked with teachers and principals in developing a process of dialogue, decision making, action, and evaluation (DDAE) which became, in fact, an indicator of ability to change. Developed to a high level, it correlated positively with the sense of personal worth, potency, and professionalism we believe must characterize the staffs of schools if they are to become dynamic, responsive institutions. Interestingly, the children in schools staffed by groups of teachers high in these traits also revealed positive attitudes toward their life in them.

Unless these conditions are present to a considerable degree in a critical mass of those adults who staff our schools, this important institution will continue to decline. We believe that further decline is not in the best interests of our democracy and the varied individuals who comprise it. Consequently, we think that the time is come to begin the reconstruction of schools by encouraging and supporting self-renewing processes within the school itself.

The laboratory for testing these ideas, the League of Cooperating Schools, was created in collaboration with eighteen school districts in southern California. The Research Division of |I|D|E|A| joined with eighteen schools in a relationship tailored to the self-interests of the two sets of partners. The *quid pro quo* was that we would help the schools help themselves if we, in turn, would have free access to the schools for purposes of documenting what problems they encountered, what cycles they went through, and what approaches they used in the process.

What happened and what we learned is described elsewhere: in a series of films available from |I|D|E|A|, 5335 Far Hills Avenue, Dayton, Ohio, and several volumes published by McGraw-Hill. The present volume reflects the total experience, including the research, but is not primarily a report on either the League or the research findings. Rather, this book is an attempt at pulling together some insights about the nature of schools, the context of schooling, and the change process for those who work in and close to schools: teachers, principals, middle-managers, and superintendents.

The premises about the reconstruction of schooling are essentially those cited above. A basic assumption is that those closely connected with schools, preoccupied as they are with their daily functioning, need to develop a better understanding of the circumstances surrounding the conduct and improvement of schools. Several chapters are directed to this end; in this respect the volume is a kind of compendium for the practitioner, with a great deal of useful information packed into a small space. A great deal of material has been drawn from sources not always familiar or available to those on the firing line and is presented in a clear, straightforward fashion.

Of greatest importance, however, is the implicit charge to those who serve in and around schools: Whatever the source, substance, and direction of the rhetoric of school reform, in the final analysis the improvements actually effected will result from the commitment and energy of the educational work force. Further, those in the schools are capable, *under certain conditions,* of reconstructing their institutions and, in the final analysis, will be held accountable. A drive for improvement must come from within and join with responsible interests from without.

The authors, Kenneth A. Tye and Jerrold M. Novotney, write out of respect for and close association with those to whom their book is addressed. Both played key roles in our work with the League. Both continue to work with |I|D|E|A| in the conduct of a major project growing directly out of our previous project—a mapping of what goes on in a sample of schools and of the changes most urgently needed. This new work will be reported at periodic intervals throughout the decade.

Although the present volume stands by itself, needing no support from the others in the Change series, the reader is urged to turn to at least some of the other volumes in seeking full understanding of the processes of school improvement to which this full body of work has led us. Richard C. Williams, Charles C. Wall, W. Michael Martin, and Arthur Berchin describe the use of a social systems approach for improving schools in *Effecting Organizational Renewal in Schools.* More than a dozen of our colleagues write on issues, difficulties, and processes inherent in the self-renewing school in *The Power to Change* (edited by Carmen M. Culver and Gary J. Hoban). A group of the teachers with whom we worked write exuberantly of their experiences with individualizing instruction in *Teachers on Individualization* (edited by David A. Shiman, Carmen M. Culver, and Ann Lieberman). Mary M. Bentzen and her associates describe the internal processes of school staffs at work with particular attention to DDAE, in *Changing Schools: The Magic Feather Principle.* My own book, *The Dynamics of Educational Change: Toward Responsive Schools,* drawing from the others, endeavors to set the entire project within the context of the last quarter century of American education and to lay out strategies for reconstructing that institution we call school for today and tomorrow.

The above speaks to a team effort involving literally hundreds who were intimately involved and many more who were in some way associated with us. Their work provides the backdrop for what you are about to read.

Although familiarity with the other volumes would be of considerable help in grasping the full story of this unique collaborative effort involving schools and the |I|D|E|A| research staff, this book is sufficiently unique and self-contained to be fully comprehended without recourse to the others. It fills a special niche in that it directs the attention of those on the firing line to what they must understand and, indeed, do if schools are to move effectively and productively from one era into another. Schools, with society, always are in transition. It behooves us to gain greater control over those human processes most likely to effect the transition smoothly. Our problem is less change than the management of it.

John I. Goodlad

ACKNOWLEDGMENTS

The authors of this volume are deeply indebted to a number of individuals who gave freely of their time and talent. M. Frances Klein and Gary J. Hoban aided immeasurably in defining the challenges of the future to be faced by our nation's schools. The fruit of our joint efforts served as the foundation for Chapter 2. Likewise, discussion with Mary M. Bentzen regarding change strategies and a review of the literature by Diana Hiatt provided a basis for Chapters 6 and 7.

Lillian K. Drag, our professional librarian, patiently answered our questions and brought pertinent literature and research findings to our attention. In the early stages of our writing, Carmen M. Culver gave us valuable editorial assistance. Later, Judith S. Golub assisted us through the critical stages of organizing, delimiting, and clarifying content. To John I. Goodlad, our thanks for his encouragement and his recognizing that "we had a book." Credit for the preparation of numerous drafts and the final manuscript is due our splendid support staff. Particular thanks go to Masako Oshita and Elizabeth Tietz and to Martha T. Twelvetree, our office manager, who always saw to it that the work got done.

In many respects we have relied upon work of others in the field, particularly Ronald Havelock. Data sources of significant practical help were the principals of the League of Cooperating Schools and the countless administrators participating in Project Leadership sponsored by the Association of California School Administrators (ACSA) under the leadership of Dr. Edward Beaubier.

Finally, without the forbearance and support of our spouses, Marilyn Tye and Patricia Novotney, we could not have completed the task. To all mentioned here and to the numerous others who encouraged and assisted us, we express our most sincere thanks.

SCHOOLS IN TRANSITION:
THE PRACTITIONER AS CHANGE AGENT

CHAPTER 1

THE AMERICAN SCHOOL TODAY: AN OVERVIEW

We live in an era of invention and innovation that has tended to make the concept of permanence as obsolete as yesterday's newspaper. The stress of our day is on the new and the unique. The man of the hour is the one who can deal most efficiently with the chaos and ambiguity of an environment that appears to be in a constant state of becoming. Not only must he be creative and original in his thinking, but he must display the ability to cast off the present or the past with the agility of a jackrabbit fleeing the fox. He who best understands, lives with, and directs change not only survives the hassle of daily existence but tends to rise to the heights of leadership. This is no less true in education than in other fields.

So much has been written about educational change that one might well question the need for yet another book on the subject. However, when the writings in the field are examined, one can readily see that there is need for a new kind of book. For example, it has become extremely popular to write books about how bad our schools have become.[1] Such books may be helpful in that they point out many of the obvious deficiencies in our schools, but they do not adequately take into account the complexities and realities of educational change processes. Also, they often provide only hazy suggestions on strategies that can be employed to bring about needed changes. Other change-oriented writings are prescriptive in nature, advocating given changes which the authors suggest should be made in schooling. These recommended changes may be in purpose, management procedures, organization or finance, curriculum, or instructional practices. As with the writings of the critics, the writings of the "advocates of practice" tend to overlook the complexities and realities of educational change proc-

1

esses. For example, those who advocate "open classrooms" or empirical models of teaching often overlook such factors as community attitudes, teacher preparation, time needed for conversion, lack of materials, finance, or legislative restrictions.

There is also a body of written material dealing with educational change which can be labeled as research or theory. Such material reveals where schools are doing less than desired and gives direction on practices that can be successful in given situations. However, many of the research and theoretical writings having to do with educational change tend to be too esoteric for the practitioner. That is, they are directed toward a limited audience of other researchers and theoreticians and have limited meaning for practitioners, which is indeed unfortunate since they can offer many insights into bringing about educational change. The problem is further complicated in that educational practitioners are so bombarded with both pressures and information and so overwhelmed by their problems that they have difficulty defining their own roles and finding "catchhold places" where they can begin to attempt to bring about the changes that are needed in schools.

Our purpose here is to draw from the existing literature on educational change to assist practitioners in defining their roles as change agents, to assist them in understanding the school as a unit undergoing change, and to provide some perspective to guide them as they consider making changes. For two reasons, we believe that *lasting educational change will come about only when practitioners see themselves as change agents*. First, there are not enough "new" people who can be trained and added on to the educational system to perform the change-agent role. Second, and more important, change is a process— a process of self-renewal, which involves seeking and finding new information, giving new meaning to such information, and acting upon this new meaning. An outside change agent can stimulate people to search for new information. He can provide such information. He can even assist people to gain new meaning. He cannot himself give new meaning to information, however, nor can he act for others.

We also believe that the most viable unit for promoting and directing educational change is the single school,[2] not the classroom or the district or the state system. While all educational agencies are important in the educational change process, only the single school has an "organismic wholeness" made up of a body politic—teachers and principal, materials and equipment, and students.[3] It is in the single school that the practitioner can initiate the process of self-renewal and ultimately where it must take place.

Unfortunately, this is not the view held by large segments of the professional and lay communities, as demonstrated by the countless number of new terms appearing almost daily on the educational scene: accountability, systems planning, planning-programming-budgeting systems (PPBS), guaranteed performance contracting, voucher plans, relevancy, franchise schools, free schools, storefront schools, community action, teacher power, and student power. As varied as these terms seem, they all have at least two things in common. First, they address the topic of educational change. Second, they arise out of an assumption that the public schools as they are now organized cannot or will not change and that outside people, be they businessmen, parents, the socially disenfranchised, or utopians, can and should make the changes —whatever such changes might be.

Pressures on educators and the educational system are nothing new. Neither is educational change. However, we live in a period of time when communication is much more open. Our problems, our needs, our potentials, and our shortcomings bombard us daily from the media. Further, our mounting social problems—population, pollution, inflation, energy, war, alienation—cause us to turn to our social institutions for help and for solutions. The schools are a convenient target.

We believe that educational practitioners want to do their part in dealing with the problems and needs of society and that they wish to change their schools to make them more responsive to these needs and problems. We agree with Charles Silberman when he says that ". . . by and large, teachers, principals and superintendents are decent, intelligent, and caring people who try to do their best. . . ."[4] We do not agree with Mr. Silberman, however, when he says that the basic problem with practitioners is their "mindlessness." On the contrary, our experience indicates that practitioners are mindful of the pressures, the problems, the faults, the alternatives, and even the research on schooling and are deeply concerned about the purposes of education. We think that one of the main obstacles which prevents practitioners from having more and better alternatives at their disposal is the gap between theory and research on the one hand and practice on the other. Researchers and theoreticians, for the most part based in universities, win recognition and advancement through conducting research and writing theoretical articles, monographs, and books. Their research and writings are judged for scholarship by fellow researchers and theoreticians. They are seldom, if ever, judged on the basis of how much they can assist practitioners in their day-to-day efforts to improve schooling.

This book is written for practitioners: teachers, principals, administrators, and intermediate agency personnel. It is not prescriptive in nature; it is not a "how to do it" book. Instead the attempt here is to bring together information pertinent to the concerns of an educational change agent in a form which can be quickly assimilated and which will open to the practitioner new areas of consideration.

THE PURPOSES OF SCHOOLING

Thut has said, "It is the nature of man to want for his children the very best that he can provide."[5] He suggests that beyond provision for physical needs, we desire to transmit to our children the "best" in the form of our beliefs, and concludes, "What a man really believes, therefore, is frequently more clearly revealed in what he teaches his children than in what he professes in public statement."[6]

Education has always been an essential thread in the fabric of American culture. From our country's beginning, our society has viewed the educative process as the key to personal and national improvement. Formal education or self-education, for the most part, seemed to pave the way to higher social status and economic gain. The prominent people of the early communities, whether clergy or laymen, were often those who could read and write or who possessed learned abilities not shared by other members of the community. Very early in our history, it became the custom to gather the younger members of the community together to instruct them formally in groups. Whether the subject matter was secular or religious, these gatherings provided a vehicle for helping the next generation benefit from the experience of the preceding.

Schools and educators later took on the task of preparing children for adult life and all that it entailed. The length of school exposure varied from individual to individual and community to community, but always the intent was the same—to pass on the religious or cultural heritage and to prepare children to be "better" or more skilled adults. The stress on the availability of schooling to all gave birth to a formal educational system that assured at least the possibility for every child to become a leader or to better his lot. As our culture turned from agricultural to industrial, the acquisition of industrial skills provided the means of escaping from the rural environs to the higher salaries of the urban manufacturing plants. As the industrial revolution progressed, education then became the means for escaping the horrors of the industrial sweatshop. Child-labor laws released countless numbers of children and youth from the factories and the fields to make use of the educational opportunities provided by a nation which had come to see the advantages and even the necessity of a literate populace.

At the same time, our schools were charged with the task of bringing into the mainstream of American life the vast numbers of immigrants from around the world who were flooding our shores. Recently, we have extended the notion of universal education by focusing attention on hitherto forgotten or marginal segments of the population. Both law and court decisions have called for equality of educational opportunity for all regardless of social class, ethnic or religious background, race, or wealth. For today's disadvantaged, as for yesterday's immigrants, the schools have been cast as a "melting pot" for the acculturation of all citizens to a common set of values and beliefs about the "American" way of life.

As a result of this history, we have come to the basic and widespread agreement that the primary purpose of schooling has been to transmit the knowledge, beliefs, and culture of our society or segments of that society to the young. Thus, we have built curricula which teach American history, geography, and government on the one hand and such skills as language mastery, mathematics, physical movement, and driving an automobile on the other. Further, we have tended to put these skills into a vocational and, of late, career-education framework. In addition, an almost hidden but very real curriculum of holiday celebrations, flag salutes, patriotic songs, and other rituals has grown up over the years as a strong mechanism for carrying out the acculturation function of schooling.[7] We hope that those who attend our schools will learn to be both good citizens—in the sense that they follow the rules of society—and contributing citizens—in the sense that they be gainfully employed.

For several decades, there has been much discussion about and even some effort to develop another purpose for schooling—improving our way of life. This movement can be dated to the famous question posed by George Counts before the Progressive Education Association in 1932: "Dare the schools build a new social order?" In a contemporary vein, Gardner answered in the affirmative when he said, "We all know in our bones that over the long haul what we do in education has the greatest relevance to building the kind of society we want."[8] Thus, our schools are seen as a means to alleviate poverty, and there has been a considerable amount of effort to equalize educational opportunity by granting large sums of money to schools serving dis-advantaged populations. We have also seen efforts to integrate our schools. We have added problem-centered curricula and socially rele-vant curricula such as sex education, family-life education, and life-adjustment education. Finally, we have seen discussion of, and some movement toward, making critical thinking or inquiry skills the heart of all school activities, since these seem to be the key skills needed if we are, in fact, to improve our way of life.

The purposes of schooling mentioned thus far—passing on the culture and extending it to all and improving our way of life—can be thought of as the societal purposes of schooling. In addition, the schools are increasingly being given the responsibility of developing the individual to his or her full potential because, as a nation, we value the worth and dignity of the individual. The means that have been em-ployed by schools to carry out this purpose have been varied and are widely in evidence. We use the learner as a data source, we diagnose and prescribe, we have independent study, we stress interest and motivation, we counsel, we involve the learner in decision making, we do away with grades, and we use programmed and other individual-ized materials.

Societal values serve as the data source for the purposes of school-ing. However, such value statements do not always tell us directly about what those purposes should be or how schools should be orga-nized to meet those purposes. Furthermore, in a society as diverse as ours, societal values are often in conflict with each other. This conflict can create a similar conflict among the purposes of schooling and, further, can easily bring confusion to planned change. The value state-ment ". . . all men are created equal . . ." in the second sentence of the Declaration of Independence and the deep-rooted value we as a peo-ple place upon "freedom of choice" often seem to be in conflict in the matter of desegregation. For example, to meet the purposes of passing on the culture to all students and developing each individual student to his fullest potential, a school district can develop a bussing plan or a boundary redistricting plan as a means to "create equality of educa-tional opportunity." On the other hand, those who subscribe to the same purposes, but who value "freedom of choice," will oppose bus-sing and redistricting and instead support open-enrollment plans and neighborhood schools. In dealing with such thorny, contradictory is-sues, the school districts, whether they know it or not, are attempting to "create a new social order." And in so doing, they may have to go it alone since neither our legislative nor our judicial bodies have seen fit to deal directly or finally with the inherent value conflict.

Describing the purposes of schooling in so brief a manner as has been done here is risky, for the relationship between the greater society and what is done in our schools is indeed a very complex one.[9] It involves such diverse factors as industrialization, technology, marriage, family, religion, the economy, foreign affairs, and our personal values. However, for the purposes of this book, it is enough to suggest that schools, school districts, and public education are systems which reside in and are responsive to greater societal systems: neighborhood, community, state, nation, and, nowadays, the world. As such, they must successfully interact with these larger systems. Further, they must assist the larger systems in the clarification of educational purposes and perhaps even societal purposes. Without such clarification, schools will tend to wander aimlessly, accomplishing poorly if at all any set of purposes other than providing custodial care for young people while parents are involved elsewhere.

The level of American economic achievement and technical advance testifies to the wisdom of our national commitment to universal public education. By and large, our schools have served us well. However, as society has become more complex and as schooling has become available to a majority of the citizenry, the school's deficiencies have been accentuated. Where once the one-room schoolhouse could provide as much intellectual stimulation and challenge as the local society could tolerate, it has become obvious that the highly bureaucratized and organized school systems of today cannot possibly meet all the needs of our children. As we strive to meet the purposes described above, a new definition of the school and its role in society is clearly needed.

As Goodlad has pointed out, we must move to differentiate clearly between education and social engineering.[10] Education should not be seen as the short-term answer to all of mankind's problems; it must not be expected to provide immediate solutions to the problems of slum clearance, of unemployment, or of public health. This is the work of social engineering—which can utilize the knowledge already provided by education. Confusion of education with social engineering contributed significantly to the disillusionment that arose when the "Great Society" so earnestly sought in the 1960s did not materialize, even though considerable sums of money were injected into the educational bloodstream.

We must also differentiate between education and schooling. In today's society, the educated person is obviously not the product of schooling alone. For example, the effects of the now commonplace radio and television and their almost universal impact on the educational process can only be guessed at. Certainly, these effects are far from minimal. Where once it was possible to live in a rural area and be untouched by the happenings beyond the local village limits, today there is scarcely a place to which one can retreat and remain unscathed by events on the opposite side of the globe. Modern man is, willingly or not, subject to a vast number of potent external forces which serve to shape his knowledge and his life. Of these, the school is only one.

The school is a human entity with institutional parameters maintained under the control of the community for specific purposes. As such, the school takes its place beside other service systems, such as those providing for fire protection, law enforcement, or community health. Its focus, however, is less easily specified in that its walls encompass a conglomeration of human beings with diverse personalities, backgrounds, and capabilities, each seeking consciously or not to gather to self the skills needed to continue to exist with some degree of comfort and happiness in a relatively formidable and unsympathetic world. Clearly, the school cannot be all things to all people. This being the case, we are inevitably faced with the question of what the school can reasonably be expected to contribute to a human being's education as the world moves into what will likely be an even more complex future.

PLAN OF THIS BOOK

Our purpose in this book is to provide an overview of the factors involved in educational change and to suggest strategies which could be used in overcoming obstacles to change in schools. Most of what we discuss has been presented in some form elsewhere, and for those who desire to go more deeply into any particular aspect, our footnotes will indicate where further information may be found. We believe, though, that this is the first time that all the facets of work on change have been drawn together for use by the practitioner.

Since change is necessarily from something to something, we begin with a projection of what the future is likely to hold and a discussion of how the anticipated changes in society will require corresponding changes in the functions and characteristics of schools. Chapter 2 provides both a justification for the need to change and some idea of the direction to take.

We turn next, in Chapters 3 and 4, to the school itself, examining the forces and influences, both internal and external, which shape it. Because we propose to deal with the school as a whole and not with the individual teacher in the classroom or a group of subject specialists, it is important to understand that the school is a complex entity composed of social interactions bounded by regulations and restrictions. If these factors are ignored, even the most intensive change effort is doomed to failure.

In Chapter 5, we turn to the concept of change itself and consider theories of why and how organizations change. Problems of *educational* change are considered in detail and obstacles to change are pointed out. Then, Chapters 6 and 7 discuss both current and emerging strategies for bringing about change in schools. We try to be as specific as possible in pointing out exactly how the strategies can be implemented, the strengths and weaknesses of each, and the types of situations in which each can be most useful. Again, footnotes provide guidance for those desiring further information.

Chapter 8 speaks directly to the various practitioners addressed in this book—superintendents, middle managers, principals, and teachers—offering recommendations for steps to be taken toward developing self-renewing schools. On the basis of the information provided in previous chapters, we hope that this chapter will provide the practitioner with a plan of action and the enthusiasm to begin.

NOTES

1   A minimal reading list would include the following: Martin Mayer, *The Schools,* Harper & Row, New York, 1961; Paul Goodman, *Compulsory Mis-Education,* Horizon Press, New York, 1965; Nat Hentoff, *Our Children Are Dying,* Viking, New York, 1965; John Holt, *How Children Fail,* Dell, New York, 1965; George Leonard, *Education and Ecstasy,* Delacorte Press, New York, 1968; Neil Postman and Charles Weingartner, *Teaching as a Subversive Activity,* Dell, New York, 1969; Charles Silberman, *Crisis in the Classroom: The Remaking of American Education,* Random House, New York, 1970; Ivan D. Illich, *Celebration of Awareness: A Call for Institutional Revolution,* Doubleday, Garden City, N.Y., 1970.

2   See also Mary M. Bentzen and Associates, *Changing Schools: The Magic Feather Principle,* McGraw-Hill, New York, 1974.

3   John I. Goodlad, "The Individual School and Its Principal: Key Setting and Key Person," *Educational Leadership,* vol. 13, p. 2, October 1956.

4   Charles E. Silberman, "Murder in the Schoolroom," *Atlantic Monthly,* vol. 225, no. 6, p. 83, June 1970.

5   I. N. Thut, *The Story of Education,* McGraw-Hill, New York, 1957, p. 16.

6   Ibid.

7   Research on the effects of political socialization by the school has shown it to be highly effective. See, for example, Fred I. Greenstein, *Children and Politics,* Yale, New Haven, Conn., 1965; and Robert D. Hess and Judith V. Torney, *The Development of Political Attitudes in Children,* Aldine, Chicago, 1967.

8   John Gardner, *No Easy Victories,* Harper & Row, New York, 1968, p. 67.

9   The historical development of the purposes of schooling can be explored in such works as Lawrence A. Cremin, *The Transformation of the School,* Vintage Books, Random House, New York, 1961; Theodore Brameld, *The Climactic Decades,* Praeger, New York, 1970; and Raymond P. Harris, *American Education: Facts, Fancies and Folklore,* Random House, New York, 1961.

10   John I. Goodlad, M. Frances Klein, Jerrold M. Novotney, Kenneth A. Tye, and Associates, *Toward a Mankind School: An Adventure in Humanistic Education,* McGraw-Hill, New York, 1974, chap. 1.

CHAPTER 2
CHALLENGES OF THE FUTURE: AN AGENDA FOR ACTION

The world has changed drastically within the life-span of most of those reading this volume. Atomic energy, space flight, computers, and satellite communication were all within the realm of science fiction less than thirty years ago. Social changes have been as rapid. The civil rights movement, the sexual revolution, women's liberation, and many other phenomena that we take for granted were new and startling to our parents. There is no reason to expect that the pace of change will slacken in the next twenty-five years. There will be indeed a "new world" in the twenty-first century. For those of us charged with educating the generations that will live in that century, the challenge is great. We must prepare children not only to cope with today's world but also to meet the opportunities of tomorrow's.

Fortunately, we are not without help as we attempt to project the kind of world for which our children will have to be prepared and the kind of schools which will have to be developed. A number of "futurists" and several agencies dedicated to long-range projection have provided us with a framework for tomorrow that affords us insight not only into the kind of society we will likely live in but into the challenges we will meet because of technical and research productivity.[1] Clearly, the world of tomorrow will present new problems and new challenges for students and educators alike.

CHANGES IN SOCIETY

Over the past thirty years, the pace of life has increased appreciably. More people go more places in less time and under greater constraints on their time. The age of TV dinners, of quick, prepackaged everything is now a reality. The stability afforded by the "family homestead" has given way to the mobile home, apartment dwelling, and frequent moves to other temporary quarters. We have become what Toffler calls a "throwaway" society[2] wherein impermanence rather than permanence is the common denominator of life. The result has been a gradual deterioration in human relations. Almost unanimously, those who write of the future see a continuation and very possibly an increase in the spirit of alienation that currently permeates our society. The dependence upon family and neighbors, so prevalent in the agrarian culture of the past, began to give way in the early part of this century to an isolationism that causes many people to feel distant from the traditional sources of culture. The fact that many of our people are seeking a solution in new living arrangements, whether in a commune, a condominium complex, or a retirement community, is an indication that we are seeking new sources of identity.

The future role of the family is not clearly perceptible, though most futurists believe it will remain similar to the present. The current trend toward communal living is not expected to last. However, Toffler suggests that family structure may be altered by a change in marriage practices.[3] He suggests that family life will be characterized by serial monogamy where one person has several partners over the course of a lifetime, rather than the traditional permanent monogamy. Even now, one or two or even three marriages are not uncommon in some circles of society. Should such a situation become more common, family life will be somewhat less stable, and it may fall to some other social institution—such as the school—to fill the gap.

Closely allied to the question of the future of the family are the changes associated with emerging new roles for women in our society. As women tend to pursue their own careers and interests apart from the home and family circle, the family relationship as traditionally understood undoubtedly will be altered still more. Increased acceptance of abortion and the use of better forms of contraception as means for family limitation will further increase woman's freedom and, consequently, cause a further alteration in the woman's role in the family. The result could well be, as Richard Flacks observes, "a serious cultural revolution."[4] An interesting prediction comes from Margaret Mead, who suggests that in the future parenthood may become an institutionalized profession, with some couples designated as parents not only of their own children but of those born to others. New government agencies may have to be created to take over the traditional duties of parents whose roles have seriously changed.

For the generations raised during the past seventy years, work was viewed as the means to financial and social success; in other words, work had taken on more than just survival value. The traditional value system of American culture prized the individual who "by the sweat of his brow" achieved prominence and stature. In an agrarian culture, and to some extent for men in the industrial context, the "hard" worker or at least "steady" worker who labored forty, fifty, or more hours a week was considered a "good" man. It appears that this value also is in the process of erosion. The demand for a shortened work week is familiar at the union contract-negotiating table. While the 37½-hour work week is not uncommon, the demand is for a still shorter week in some industries, and the "guaranteed wage" is a distinct possibility. In addition, various energy shortages may necessitate a three- or four-day work week. The past ten years have witnessed a trend toward earlier retirement from formal occupations, a greater desire for varied work experience, a tendency among some groups to switch professions at middle age, and greater pressure for creation of adult-education opportunities. Undoubtedly, these trends will continue.

The problem which concerns some futurists is whether people will be able to adapt to having greater free time at their disposal. Preparation for worthwhile use of increased leisure will become the direct responsibility of educators. Colm has said, "I believe it would be wrong to conclude that we should replace our philosophy of work by one of non-work, . . . but we should supplement education for the work that needs to be done with education for a gradual increase in the opportunities for nonremunerative but useful activities."[5]

Other futurists question whether there will be a need to work at all. Education in our country always has been regarded as the means by which individuals either became responsible citizens or got "good" jobs or both. As job opportunities decrease for the well-educated (particularly in times of economic stress), it may well be that education will become an end in itself, and that provision by the government of a guaranteed annual wage will allow many to spend their entire lives gainfully involved in the educative process.

Regardless of the ultimate outcome of changes in the area of leisure and work, clearly the whole question of the "work ethic" will have to be reexamined. We will have to be alert to the possibility of the demise of one ethic and, hopefully, the birth of a suitable replacement.

The work ethic cannot be discussed without touching at least briefly on economic trends that already are evident. It is obvious that as the present century draws to a close, greater quantities of food and manufactured products will be produced by fewer people. Within recent years, the Labor Department has indicated that as many as 40,000 jobs are being eliminated each week by the installation of automated manufacturing devices. It is a fact that less than one-quarter of our population now produces the food for the entire nation. There is nothing to indicate that these trends will not continue. Service industries and occupations will continue to increase in numbers and size. Basic economic questions will have to do with the distribution of wealth both within the nation and worldwide and with the role that government will play in guaranteeing such a distribution. Full employment, taxes, government spending for education and other social services, social security, control of inflation, and foreign aid are all economic issues which must be dealt with over the next thirty years and which are tied to the distribution of wealth.

Speculation about the political future of our country covers a broad spectrum. Writers such as Daniel Moynihan, David Elazar, and Andrew Hacker believe that the year 2000 will witness a highly bureaucratized, more centralized federal government than we have today. Others such as Richard Flacks and Lawrence Frank see a much more open system with government at all levels responsive to the needs of individuals and much more tolerant of a wide array of social and cultural values and life-styles. The American political scene in the year 2000 may be characterized by both more centralized government and more individual freedom.

One arena of political action will concern the integration of minority groups into the political, economic, and social life of the nation. It is unlikely that minority groups will become less vocal in their demand for total equality in the national decision-making processes, in the economy, and in the society at large. Minority groups, whether categorized along racial lines or by other distinctions (such as homosexuals, students, the elderly) or by ideological or moral positions (such as ecologists or women's liberationists), will continue to demand their rights. As in the recent past, it will ultimately fall to the government, both national and local, to alleviate the tensions that will arise when concessions are granted to or won by minorities.

When we consider the economic and political future of this nation, we cannot ignore the fact that there will be a continued growth in worldwide interdependence. The stark realities of war, hunger, pollution, and limited resources demand it. Improvements in communications and transportation technology make it possible. The growth and perseverance of multinational corporations and international social, scientific, legal, and political organizations herald it. Our dealings in the next thirty years in our own nation with questions of distribution of wealth, centralization of government, and individual freedom will be a rehearsal for dealing with them on a global basis in the twenty-first century.

SCIENCE AND TECHNOLOGY

Speculating about the world of tomorrow in terms of science and technology is somewhat less difficult or at least less risky than speculating in the realm of values or social structure. While all aspects of each field cannot be adequately covered here, an examination of contributions from biomedics, computer technology, communication, transportation, architecture, and urban planning—these last in relation to population projections—will provide the broad brush strokes for a general view of tomorrow.

Turning first to the field of biomedics, one is struck by the endless possibilities for speculation on the physical nature of tomorrow's human being. The vast amount of research currently being done in genetics shows that genetic manipulation is more than a possibility. During the last decade, mutations have been produced in microorganisms in a nonrandom fashion. Delgado predicts that as science unravels the genetic code, it will become possible to control heredity, offering the prospect of eliminating hereditary diseases and producing individuals with certain desirable physical or mental characteristics.[6]

Not only will genetic manipulation offer the possibility of eliminating hereditary or mutational disease, but prospects are real for the elimination of traits and characteristics seen as undesirable by large groups of people. It may even be possible to produce human beings to order through techniques such as cloning or nuclear transplantation. Such a possibility presents moral and ethical questions of immeasurable dimensions.

In the area of extrauterine fertilization, attempts are being made to allow human embryos to develop outside the female womb for later implantation in surrogate mothers or simply for scientific observation. Predictions are that such procedures may be perfected within as few as twenty or thirty years. The possibility of raising a generation of children with only one or possibly even no true functioning parents is very real. What impact this will have on family life and love relationships is not at all certain, but as in the field of genetics, a completely new set of ethical and moral problems may be just beyond the horizon.

Simultaneous with research into the beginning of life, work is being done to unlock the secrets of the aging process and to improve our knowledge of preventive medicine. The average life expectancy of the United States resident is already considerably above what it was fifty years ago. Greater efficiency in warding off disease, joined with greater knowledge in slowing the process of aging, will result in a society with larger numbers of elderly people. Census statistics indicate that this trend already is evident.

Drugs and other methods of behavior modification and control present both threat and promise for the future. On the one hand, already massive problems of drug abuse can be expected to increase as new drugs are developed and advertising promotes their use. There is also the problem of who is to control behavior-manipulating techniques. On the other hand, Gordon suggests that drugs and other methods of behavior control could enhance a retardate's ability to learn, stimulate cognitive growth in children, and control deviant and criminal behavior.[7]

Recent drug experiments have found that memory storage involves a complex system of processes which, if understood more fully, might provide the ability to correct biochemically based deficiencies of learning and memory.[8] It might even be possible to transfer some learned activities from one individual to another, and we can foresee a time when students who are about to enter the period of formal schooling will receive a learning shot along with their immunization shots to increase both motivation and capacity for learning. If the motivation problem were solved in this way, and if teaching machines and computers which are now being developed were really able to move into the educational process, the age of educational technology would be fully upon us, for better or for worse.

Computer technology also holds great promise for the future as an aid to people in performing their less desirable and routine tasks. One has but to visit a steel-rolling mill in which all operations are monitored by one man at the control board of a computer or a billing agency where collating, computating, and printing are done by computer to see now what has been predicted to be widespread in the future. It is obvious that computer technology will play an increasingly important part in every segment of human existence as the twenty-first century dawns.

The advance of communication techniques is closely linked with advances in computer technology. Even today, computer vote-profile analyses are quickly communicated to a mass audience via network television, and election winners are predicted before the polls have closed. The interaction of telephone equipment with television and satellite have already caused the globe to shrink, and all the evidence indicates that by the year 2000 it will be a simple thing to put complicated yet very reliable electronic communication equipment anywhere. As cable television becomes more common, no part of the country will be inaccessible or remote. A cultural homogenization may well result.

Futurists also predict rapid advances in the field of transportation. Toffler talks of clogged freeways, overcrowded airports, and stacked flight patterns as characterizing the year 2000, though it is hoped that current concern for these very problems will lead to their solution in the relatively near future. There is little doubt that the world of tomorrow will see new approaches to mass rapid transit, enabling larger groups of people to move at faster speeds within a metropolitan area. Very likely auto traffic flow will be monitored and controlled by central traffic offices. As Feldman says:

> By the beginning of the twenty-first century, at least one new high speed, long distance transportation mode should have been developed and added to the nation's stockpile of new transportation modes. High speed systems should be speeding air travelers from all large United States airports to interfaces with local distribution systems. At least one east-west and two north-south automatic highways should be guiding and controlling individual passenger vehicles speeding from coast to coast and border to border.[9]

But more important even than local travel will be the international mobility of our populace. Countless individuals already consider the world their playground, shopping center, or place of business. The number of tourists covering the globe each year is legion. Even now, some members of the business community follow a schedule that can have them spending Monday in Manhattan, Tuesday in Paris, Wednesday in Rome, and Thursday in Cairo. Such may very well be the lot of a considerably greater number of people by the year 2000. The ramifications in terms of social values and economic and monetary considerations, as well as world health, can only be guessed. Obviously, the traditional nationalism of the nineteenth and twentieth centuries will be utterly outdated as we move into the twenty-first century.

The present trend toward urbanization is expected to continue. If predictions reach reality, the country will be characterized by large, highly urbanized metropolitan areas. Kahn and Weiner have indicated three by name: "Boswash," encompassing our present-day Boston, New York, and Washington, D.C.; "Sansan," covering the San Francisco, Los Angeles, San Diego terrain; and "Chipitts," extending from Chicago around the Great Lakes to Pittsburgh.[10] With vast urbanization will very likely come an increase in the number and size of problems the cities of today are confronting. If, as is presently the case, minority groups continue to dwell in the central areas while the white population flees to the suburbs, social inequities will be exaggerated and continued strife between these groups will be likely.

The predicted concentration of human beings has given rise to the question of how they will be housed. It is expected that new building materials and sophisticated architectural engineering skills will be developed and that new materials and construction techniques will result in a decrease in cost. A new view of the relationship between architecture, construction, and urban planning has begun to evolve, so that architects will concern themselves not only with the shape and form of the buildings they design but also with the purposes they are to serve, the time and space in which they are placed, and the psychological effects of their designs on the people who use them.

Internally, dwellings are expected to become even more functional than those currently being built. An increase in the number and flexibility of available household appliances is expected. Homes may even rely heavily on computers in their day-to-day operations.

As people live in greater numbers, in closer proximity, and in different configurations, new questions about land-use ethics will have to be confronted. As architects are beginning to see their role differently even now, so too a whole new field of concern centering upon the social dynamics of real estate almost certainly will evolve. Perhaps the realtor's responsibility will no longer cease when he sells a house. He will likely be held accountable for what occurs when he brings together a diverse group of individuals into a new community or for the consequences that result in an older community because of his introducing new or different elements or his refusal to do so. The world of tomorrow will undoubtedly demand as great a social consciousness on the part of those who plan, build, and sell new communities as it does now of those who occupy the buildings.

The multiplication of dwellings and increasing density of urban areas presumes several definite trends in population growth. Almost universally, futurists are expressing concern about population growth, some because of what they see as inevitable overpopulation and others, more recently, because of what they see as possible population decline. Bengelsdorf, for instance, predicts that by the year 2000, the United States population will rise from its current level of 208 million to 340 million.[11] More recently, government research has indicated that the population increase may be subsiding and that by the year 2000 we may be barely reproducing ourselves. A government survey found that in 1971 82 babies were born per 1,000 women as opposed to 87 babies per 1,000 women in the previous year. This was the lowest birthrate reported since 1940.

No matter which prediction comes true, adequate planning will be essential, for even if we were to stabilize our population, the effects of technological growth would still offer a threat to the environment. Undoubtedly, considerable concern and effort in the years ahead will be directed toward environmental management. The problems of water, air, and noise pollution will continue to be of paramount importance. Very likely, the last quarter of this century will witness monumental efforts to improve the environment and preserve our nation's natural resources so that man can survive.

SCHOOLS AND THE FUTURE

However one chooses to view the various predictions listed in this chapter, it is not possible to remain complacent. If even a small portion of what has been predicted comes true, the world of tomorrow will be almost unrecognizable to today's people. For the educator, the problem is clear: how can the children of today be educated to live in the world that hardly can be imagined but which will be upon us with appalling rapidity? Clearly, our traditional approach to schooling will not be adequate to handle the task, and we must begin now to restructure our educational system. The question is, what implications do these projections of the future hold for schools and in which directions should today's educators begin their planning?

Responding to Changing Patterns of Family Life

Impermanence of marriage, new roles for women, and even advances in biomedics (e.g., extrauterine fertilization) suggest that there will be a continuing decline in the importance of the family as an influence on children and youth. Thus, it can be anticipated that, along with other institutions, the school will have to take over or supplement some of the responsibilities for children which traditionally have been those of the family alone.

Three areas of change come to mind when one considers the traditional functions of the family and a shift of such functions to the school: (1) early education, (2) affective development, and (3) the presentation of sex roles in various curricula.

Where formerly children normally started school at age five or six, the trend now is toward entering them into the formal school system at a much earlier age. Headstart programs, day care centers, and even a growing private nursery school movement verify this trend. The city of Pittsburgh, for example, has attempted to bridge the gap between preschool training and the elementary school by taking fifty-eight preschool units under its jurisdiction. Children in the future may be starting their schooling as early as thirty months after birth. The question is what kind of experiences should be provided in programs of early education? Clearly, the mere extension downward of traditional first grade and kindergarten readiness programs emphasizing the alphabet, numbers, and other content will be inadequate. Likewise, it is clear that the unfocused programs of play, music, stories, and passes at the alphabet and numbers found in a large number of nursery schools will also be inadequate.[12] Goodlad observed about the goals of early schooling that:

> . . . never-failing adult support and a set of guiding values need to be infused into every activity. For the early phase of schooling, the values to be supported are that the child achieve a sense of personal well-being expressed in his self-confident relationship with objects, peers, and adults; his lack of fear; his confrontations with his occasionally angry, hating, antisocial self; his ability to move in and out of an imaginary world in which knights fight battles with serpents and dragons and win; and his transition from narcissistic contemplation of self to interaction with an increasingly expanding environment. These are the marks of the child successfully using his early years, not his level of performance on school-oriented tests. These are the emerging attributes for which he

must have unfaltering adult support. These are the goals for the first phase of schooling.

Reading, numbers, and the like are meaningful to the degree they help the child achieve these goals—and very meaningful, indeed, they can be, because they are the tools of the human race that extend self-transcendence in limitless ways. But they are not the goals of early schooling. Unfortunately, it is mistaking these mundane means for the ends of education that has corrupted schooling at all levels. Early schools have the best opportunity and the most serious responsibility for maintaining at all times the necessary distinction.[13]

While support and guidance will be critical for the very young, it will also be critical for older children and youth in a time of declining family stability. The schools of tomorrow must focus at all levels on providing new opportunities for pupil self-fulfillment in line with the need to prepare children to become humane, self-renewing, self-directed individuals who will not only survive in society, but who will take a conscious role in shaping it for the better.[14] What is implied here is a strong humanistic orientation for schools wherein the learner will be accepted for what he is and given the freedom to be what he can become.

Such a view of the student will require a revision of the content in the schools of the future. The Center for the Study of Instruction of the National Education Association suggests:

The curriculum must move away from an emphasis on the retention of facts to emphasis on the processes of inquiry, comparison, interpretation, and synthesis. In addition to purely intellectual growth, the curriculum should regard emotions, ideals, ambitions, and values as legitimate areas of concern for the educational process and should emphasize a student's need to develop a sense of respect for self and others. Such a curriculum demands a reordering of the priorities of the school and any instructional program which will be reflective of the new order.[15]

One current movement which affords promise in terms of the need for a more humanistic orientation is the creation of middle schools. Historically, the junior high school was created to bridge the gap between elementary and high school. Its functions were to be exploration, guidance, and remediation. With its large numbers, frequent class changes, and emphasis upon subject matter, however, it has become, in many instances, a watered-down senior high school. Middle schools, at least the good ones, seem to be designed to provide an environment in which the preadolescent can more easily determine who he is through contact with a wide variety of programs which allow him to explore his intellectual, aesthetic, social, personal, and career abilities and options.

The family, by and large, has provided a supportive climate for children and youth, one in which their self-concepts have been able to develop in a positive manner. Likewise, it has always provided parental and sibling models. If the school is to assume some of the responsibilities traditionally held by family, it is logical to conclude that the development of a supportive climate and the presentation of healthy models will be important tasks for tomorrow's schools. In this regard, it is interesting to note that in one study, a strong relationship was found between the attitudes toward learning, attitudes toward school, and the self-concepts of upper elementary school pupils and a school climate wherein teachers are involved significantly in school decision making and themselves have a sense of "power" over their own work life and space.[16] What this seems to indicate is that the affective development of students is necessarily correlated with the feelings and attitudes of the adults with whom they come in contact in the school. Thus, schools of tomorrow will be faced with a primary task of becoming "good" places for children, youth, and adults to work, learn, and live together. It is the responsibility of the practitioners now in the schools to see that their schools become such places.

The increase in the number of working mothers has an obvious impact on traditional relationships in the family. When the mother works outside the home, the father has to share domestic duties and child-rearing activities. Further, the movement of women out of the home and into jobs heretofore usually held by men (e.g., auto mechanics, lawyers, carpenters, professional athletes, managers) creates some conflict in boys and girls with regard to sex role identification. Such conflict is reinforced by the stereotypes found in current curricula and behavior norms of our schools. At the primary level, for example, it is assumed, and materials of instruction reinforce the notion, that little girls are "made of sugar and spice and everything nice." How many times have we heard girls told that "little girls don't do that kind of thing" when they are caught rough and tumbling with their male counterparts?

Sex role stereotypes are reinforced throughout the grades. At the upper elementary level, it is a foregone conclusion that girls will read library books about horses and nurses and that boys will read about sports and cars. In junior high school, boys are automatically scheduled into mechanical drawing and wood shop and girls into cooking and sewing. In high school, it is generally easy to predict who will enroll in business courses, auto mechanics, or even physics.

Today's practitioners can certainly make a start toward changing some of these practices within their schools. Later chapters will offer some suggestions about obstacles that will have to be overcome and strategies that can be employed.

Responding to Alienation

As institutions such as the family change, society's values change. The condition of being "between" old values and new ones can bring with it a state of rootlessness or even alienation in the individual who is groping to find for himself some set of guiding life principles. This is compounded by increasing mobility and the impersonal nature of our sprawling metropolitan areas. The schools of tomorrow will have a major responsibility to assist children and youth to see their place in the order of things in the world. In fact, it appears that the raison d'être of tomorrow's schools may be derived from the need of human beings of every age to be able to accept and deal with reality. If the tempo of change increases in the years ahead, the main contribution of the school to society may be in helping individuals derive stability for themselves within a constantly varying milieu.

Critical to this process will be continued concern with teaching the traditional cursive and computational skills. No other institution in our society is designed or equipped for this task or includes trained professionals who presumably have knowledge of the best ways of imparting these skills with some economy of time. The purpose of the intellectual environment of the school is the stimulation in others of the desire to acquire such skills and the maintenance and preservation of these skills. In this way, the school provides a unique service unavailable in most modern homes.

Closely allied with the computational skills, and very pertinent to the central mission of the school, is a command of the processes related to rational thinking and problem solving. The school may well find its most important task is helping students to acquire an understanding of inductive and deductive methods and the advantages of their application in a variety of situations. Since by its nature the school is dedicated to presenting challenges to students, instruction in the modes by which such problems can be handled is clearly within its mission and capability. In conjunction with instruction in problem solving, a legitimate expectation is that the school give considerable attention to the formulation of individual work habits. Ways and means of organizing large amounts of data, of formulating criteria for discarding the irrelevant, of productively utilizing time, form a significant part of such training.

Because schools bring together a varied sample of human beings, both child and adult, they reflect in some degree the society and culture in which they exist and, therefore, afford an opportunity to enhance acquisition of social skills. It is reasonable to expect schools not only to provide an opportunity to practice social behaviors but to examine their worth and preferability. Instruction in democratic processes and cooperative endeavor would naturally form a part of such an effort.

Essential to the process of accepting and dealing with reality is a recognition of one's own strengths and weaknesses. It is not unreasonable, therefore, to expect the school to help an individual to assess his potential and to create a program for maximizing innate talents. The school provides a unique and opportunely varied setting for individual comparison, and, in a nonthreatening climate, each student could be helped to view himself as others see him and to deal in the most productive way with such feedback.

The school can be expected to provide a forum for inquiry on questions raised in any other sphere of human activity. Exploring relationships and planning and implementing courses of action in the world would go a long way toward giving students a sense of belonging and of being of value to others. Social, cultural, political, and economic systems would be taken apart and examined for what they are and in light of needed improvements. The humanities, arts, and philosophy would be explored in depth and engaged in as a means of improving human communication of both ideas and emotions. Planning for the future, individually and collectively, would be practiced. As Tyler has written: "The goals of education appropriate for a future that will include many surprises will include strong emphasis on problem-solving, upon learning how to meet new situations, upon the skills of observation, analysis and communication, and upon the development of attitudes appropriate to change."[17]

The school can also reasonably be expected to instill in its students a love for learning and a sense of satisfaction when new insights are gained. Achieving what at first blush appears to be an idealistic goal would make it possible for the schools to become more than symbols of the status quo and mere channels for passage of the traditional culture to the next generation. If the spirit of inquiry were joined with a love of learning, the schools could become, as Parker says, "vehicles for continuous social evolution."[18] In a fast-changing world, such a vehicle is needed if we are to avoid a high degree of alienation and cultural "drift."

The school can also become a setting for the identification, exploration, and development of the creative and aesthetic talents possessed by each individual. Explorations in and appreciation of art, music, literature, drama, architecture, poetry, and the like can be paramount in assisting each individual to create his own identity and to identify with others throughout the world.

Lastly, the schools of tomorrow will need to consider a whole series of structural changes which will be directed toward overcoming the growing alienation of youth. The Panel on Youth of the President's Science Advisory Committee proposes a number of structural changes such as doing away with the comprehensive high school and replacing it with schools among which students may choose.[19] This, of course, calls for eliminating "fixed" geographic attendance areas. Although this kind of decision will have to be made by the society at large, practitioners in the school now can make a start toward providing for the needs of students by exploring ways to offer a variety of alternatives within the single school.

The Panel's report also recommends that the student's time in school not be spent wholly in self-centered or self-improvement activities but that opportunities be provided for interacting with and serving others. Thus, the direct teaching role of the school would be lessened while the counseling role would be increased, and students' participation in work and service experiences and extracurricular activities would be encouraged. Finally, closer cooperation with youth organizations and communities would become increasingly important. The report cautions, however, that there is need for thoughtful planning and research concerning such options, for there would be little value in schools simply jumping on some new "bandwagon."

Responding to the Need for Continuing Education

A whole host of factors related to a change in our work ethic referred to earlier suggests parallel changes in the schools of tomorrow. Because of such factors and because of the increased production of knowledge in almost every field, the schools of tomorrow will need to provide a whole range of continuing education experiences. The need to learn and the process of retraining will continue throughout most people's lives. The rapid growth of junior colleges, adult education programs, extension programs, and open universities testifies to the trend toward more continuing education experiences in number and in kind. Three types of continuing education will need to be developed more fully in the future: (1) vocational, (2) avocational, and (3) social-psychological.

Continuing *vocational* education can take many forms, such as on-the-job training and in-service training. The work-study programs for high school students can serve as a model for adults who are learning a new occupation or upgrading their skills in a current occupation. The critical point is that collaborative relationships must be developed between schools and industries which are in need of service and can provide training. Also, there must be counseling services for individuals who need to know about available opportunities and about their own aptitudes, and imaginative new uses of the media, public and commercial, must be brought into play so that learning can take place in a variety of settings.

A critical factor for secondary schools to consider is that in the future they will not be responsible for providing students with specific vocational skills. It will not be their task to judge and sort students into vocational categories. Programs such as Job Corps and the circumstances surrounding the increasing number of junior college enrollees are showing that such specific skill development and sorting have caused students to have to undo or redo the results of many of their secondary school experiences. Individual "sorting" and specific job training will become the task of continuing education. What secondary schools will have to do in the future is to provide for students a variety of exploratory experiences, personal and social development opportunities, and opportunities for the development of problem-solving skills and abilities.

Continuing education for meeting the *avocational* needs of the citizenry may include courses and subjects which might have seemed frivolous in the past, such as yoga, astrology, home repairs, bridge, golf, mountain climbing, sand-casting, theater, dieting, consumer education of various kinds, political participation, and countless other areas of interest. Three functions will be served by an expanded program of avocational offerings. First, and most obvious, each individual will benefit in that he will be able to increase his own skills. Second, individuals will be able to meet other individuals with common interests, thus counteracting the problem of alienation. Finally, it seems obvious that investment in human development as a preventive measure will go a long way toward counteracting our continual need to invest heavily in corrective mental health and criminal programs. We have given much lip service in the past to human development as a sound economic and social investment. The future will demand that we commit ourselves to such an investment, and continuing education will be an important part of that commitment.

Changing patterns of marriage, child rearing, work patterns, and the like will create a number of strains upon human beings caught between what they have learned as traditional values and behaviors and new emerging values and behaviors. Continuing social-psychological education would assist individuals as they attempt to deal with such changes in values and behaviors. Subjects such as child rearing, marriage, mid-life crisis, group living, aging, and death would become critical to any program of continuing education.

Integrating the School and Its Urban Environment

It has been estimated that 80 percent of America's children and youth will attend school in urban areas by 1980. Urbanization as a phenomenon cannot be separated from other concerns such as alienation, value conflicts, and pluralism. However, facing the reality of people living together in close proximity means facing the similar reality of the need for changes in urban schooling. In addition to a more humanistic orientation, early education, and continuing education, the schools of tomorrow will need to serve as centers for the community on the one hand and will need to extend their programs outward into the community on the other. Thus, one would see schools being used around the clock, seven days a week, as centers of continuing education and, when appropriate, as centers for social services. Likewise, plans similar to the "schools without walls" found in Philadelphia's Parkway School, Chicago's Metroplan, and New Orleans' Gateway School will become common, as will Rusch's "Mobile School."[20] Such schools search out community resources wherein pupils can learn firsthand what makes the city operate and what the city has to offer the individual as a learner. Further, schools of the future will enter into more and more cooperative arrangements with other educational agencies such as museums; institutes; labor, business, and professional groups; and the media. As the report of the White House Conference on Children pointed out:

> School as we now know it will have been replaced by a diffused learning environment involving homes, parks, public buildings, museums, business offices and guidance centers. Many such resources which are now un-endorsed, unofficial, unrecognized, unstructured or unsupervised—and unused—will be endorsed and made fully available for learning. There will be successors to our present schools—places designed for people to gather for purposes of learning things together.[21]

Also, the schools must increase dramatically the number and kind of people who are brought into the school as learning resources for children and youth. New and more varied ways will have to be devised for integration of parents into the educational mechanism. In addition, the staff of the school is likely to increase in two directions. First, there will be more highly trained people with expertise in psychology, eval-uation, curriculum materials, and school-community relations to offer assistance to the teacher. In addition, many routine tasks will be taken over by aids and volunteers, freeing the teacher to concentrate on the more professional aspects of the job.

Two additional responsibilities for our schools arise from the fact that urbanization is upon us. First, because urban schools will continue to bring together a varied sample of human beings, they reflect the society and varied cultures in which they exist. The interactions which occur in the school, if correctly structured, should lead to acquisition of social skills, tolerance, and appreciation of differences needed for urban living. The present trend toward intergroup education is one which will be expanded in tomorrow's schools.

Second, our urban environment will require much attention in the future. Concerns for housing, transportation, crime, child care, and pollution will require a great amount of human engineering. Such en-gineering always raises ethical questions. The perennial clash between the collective good and individual or small group rights will heighten in the future. Thus, while students are learning to inquire, to solve real problems, and to understand political processes, they must also learn to deal with ethical considerations and actions.[22] This includes know-ing how to determine the wants, interests, and preferences of a variety of people. It also means knowing how to use group processes of deci-sion making, including articulating these wants, interests, and prefer-ences and arriving at consensus.

Responding to a Shrinking World

There can be no doubt that our continuing advances in communication and transportation and our growing worldwide economic and political interdependence will call for changes in the schools of tomorrow. Whereas the family and the community are somewhat limited in the perspective they provide a student, the school can and should provide a worldwide backdrop against which local events can be evaluated and through which the interdependence of men can be highlighted.

To develop a worldwide perspective in students, the schools of tomorrow will have to overcome the ethnocentrism of our present curriculum. Not just Western or American culture, but literature, art, music, and history from around the world will be studied. Further, economic, political, cultural, and social structures will be examined with the purpose of finding commonalities among men, not differences which point subtly toward American superiority.[23]

Resources, including the broadcast and print media, people who have traveled to other places, and people who are visiting in the community from other places, will be utilized frequently. Exchange programs and travel programs will be encouraged for all students and teachers, regardless of family income. In short, the school will be an institution with the resources to reach across continents to deal with global concerns and to bring the commonalities of people into bold relief for all of those in the school and the community.

SUMMARY

In a time of rapid change, a society's values are often the first casualty. Old values are challenged and fall; new values have yet to reach the status of tradition. We live now in what might be called a "value vacuum," as the traditional moral arbiters such as the family, community, church, and governments are groping for new roles and new meanings in a changing world. Our schools are groping, also.

There are those who object to "change in schools for the sake of change." They are probably correct in these objections. However, our schools do need to change and they need to do so in light of the societal factors set forth in this chapter as well as in light of similar factors which will continue to emerge. It is through a constant analysis of the future and its meaning for the people who live in our society that we can begin to plan new roles, structures, and programs for our schools. These will be roles, structures, and programs which will assist us in clarifying our values and which will prepare us to live in the future.

NOTES

1   See, for example, the writings of Alvin Toffler, Charles Reich, Herman Kahn, Anthony Weiner, Marshall McLuhan, and Andrew Hacker, as well as the reports put out by the Stanford Research Institute, the Committee on Economic Development, and Educational Inquiry, Inc.

2   Alvin Toffler, *Future Shock,* Random House, New York, 1970.

3   Ibid.

4   Richard Flacks, "Strategies for Radical Social Change," *Social Policy,* March–April 1971, p. 11.

5   Gerhard Colm, "Prospective Economic Development," in *Prospective Changes in Society by 1980,* Designing Education for the Future, an Eight-State Project, Denver, 1966, p. 93.

6   Jose M. Delgado, *Physical Control of the Mind: Toward a Psycho-civilized Society,* Harper & Row, New York, 1969.

7   Theodore H. Gordon, *The Future,* Martin Press, New York, 1965.

8   See "The Chemical Transfer of Memory: Research and Implications," an |I|D|E|A| occasional paper, available from Institute for Development of Educational Activities, Inc., Information and Services Division, P.O. Box 446, Melbourne, Fla., 1970.

9   Max L. Feldman, "Transportation: An Equal Opportunity for Access," in William R. Ewald, Jr. (ed.), *Environment and Policy: The Next Fifty Years,* Indiana University Press, Bloomington, 1968, p. 173.

10   Herman Kahn and Anthony J. Weiner, *The Year 2000: A Framework for Speculation on the Next Thirty-three Years,* Macmillan, New York, 1967.

11   Irving S. Bengelsdorf, *Spaceship Earth: People and Pollution,* Fox-Mathes Publications, Los Angeles, 1969.

12   See John I. Goodlad, M. Frances Klein, Jerrold M. Novotney, and Associates, *Early Schooling in the United States,* McGraw-Hill, New York, 1973.

13   Ibid., pp. 155–156.

14   Warren T. Greenleaf and Gary A. Griffin, *Schools for the Seventies and Beyond: A Call to Action,* staff report, National Education Association, Center for the Study of Instruction, Washington, D.C., 1971.

15   Ibid., pp. 52–53.

16   Alice Z. Seeman and Melvin Seeman, "Staff Processes and Pupil Attitudes: A Study of Teacher Participation in Educational Change," unpublished paper.

17   Ralph Tyler, "Purposes, Scope and Organization of Education," in *Implications for Education of Prospective Changes in Society*, Designing Education for the Future, an Eight-State Project, Denver, 1967, p. 36.

18   Don H. Parker, *Schooling for What?* McGraw-Hill, New York, 1970.

19   James S. Coleman and others, *Youth: Transition to Adulthood*, Report of the Panel on Youth of the President's Science Advisory Committee, The University of Chicago Press, Chicago, 1974.

20   Charles Rusch, "MOBOC: A Mobile Learning Environment," in Gary Coates (ed.), *Alternative Learning Environments*, Dowden, Hutchinson, Ross, Inc., Stroudsburg, Pa., 1974.

21   White House Conference on Children, "Learning Toward A.D. 2000," Report from Forum 5, December 13–18, 1970, p. 78.

22   Questions such as these are dealt with in chaps. 3 and 4 of John I. Goodlad, M. Frances Klein, Jerrold M. Novotney, Kenneth A. Tye, and Associates, *Toward a Mankind School: An Adventure in Humanistic Education*, McGraw-Hill, New York, 1974.

23   Ibid., chap. 4, provides guidelines and suggestions.

CHAPTER 3

THE SCHOOL AS A SOCIAL SYSTEM

Schools are not islands unto themselves, although some parents who attempt to enter them in order to seek information or to make their wishes known might come away believing so. Actually, schools are systems which interact with other surrounding systems (e.g., health, welfare, and legal agencies; churches; taxpayer associations; parent groups). They are defined by more or less clear boundaries which distinguish them from the environment. A school is an open system to the degree that it interacts with its environment and the larger systems of which it is a part.

There are numerous systems models in existence, each having its theoretical roots in one or another discipline. For example, there is a social system derived from sociological theory, a cultural system derived from anthropology, an individual system derived from personality theory. Although each of these orientations emphasizes specific concepts, all open-system models have certain key concepts in common. For example, all systems have goals ranging from sheer survival to improving the welfare of the system members. Systems have boundaries which they maintain in order to remain distinguished from other systems. Such boundaries can be physical or they can be matters of custom which keep nonmembers from entering or altering a system. Also, demands are made upon systems and support is given from the outside, which the system itself can reject, or accept, and adapt to. Further, systems build structures which allow them to carry out functions which, in turn, lead to goal attainment. Ways of making decisions and communicating among members are structures, while actions carried out by system members are functions. In most systems, certain functions are reserved for specific members. Such specialization of function leads to the definition of roles. Likewise, in most systems there are behaviors which are expected of all members, such as modes of dress, speech, and seating patterns. These are norms.

These shared concepts from systems theories are helpful to us in two ways as we consider the change process in schools. First, they give us a vocabulary we can use to make comparisons across schools and between schools and other systems. Second—and this point is critical to the change process—when a change is made in one aspect of schooling, that change more than likely affects other aspects. Viewing change from a systems perspective helps us understand this fact and also can help us to do a better job as change agents by pointing to places where changes can and should be brought about.

All systems except the smallest have subsystems, and all but the largest have suprasystems to which they belong. Systems concepts are easily applied to the school. A school system is an entity that has, among other characteristics, a given staff, an identifiable governing body, given resources, and unique functions which distinguish it from other systems. It is also a subsystem of larger educational systems: the school district, the county system, or the state education system. For analytical purposes, one could also consider the subsystems of the school: departments, grade levels, teams of teachers, classrooms. In this chapter, however, the school itself is considered as the basic system.

THE INTERNAL DIMENSIONS OF THE SCHOOL

An adequate image of a school as a social system includes at least five internal dimensions: (1) institutional expectations, (2) individual needs, (3) processes, (4) informal norms, and (5) organizational complexity.

Jacob Getzels developed a theoretical framework which includes the first two dimensions and which describes the operation of schools as a series of interactions between the institutional expectations and individual needs within the school.[1] His model has become one basis for understanding and examining the social system of the school.

The *institutional dimension* corresponds roughly to the structures found in the school. These structures include procedures, patterns of doing things, rules, regulations, and policies, and they define the *roles* which should be performed by those who hold positions within the school. In most schools, such roles are rather well defined. The principal performs management functions (ordering and accounting for

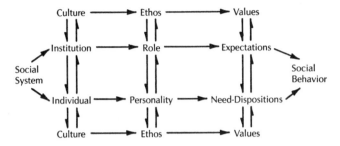

FIGURE 3.1   OPERATIONAL MODEL OF MAJOR DIMENSIONS OF SOCIAL BEHAVIOR

From J. W. Getzels, "Conflict and Role Behavior in the Educational Setting," in W. W. Charters, Jr., and N. L. Gage (eds.), *Readings in the Social Psychology of Education.* Copyright 1963 by Allyn and Bacon, Inc. Reprinted by permission of the publisher.

books and supplies, budgeting, and distributing and checking various teacher reporting forms) and leadership functions, such as presiding at staff meetings, reviewing and approving teachers' instructional plans, and serving as the ultimate decision-making authority in the school. In addition, he or she mediates between students, teachers, district personnel, parents, and the community at large. The typical school also contains a number of teachers who are roughly equal, each of whom works behind a classroom door with a single group of students. They typically have responsibility for the learnings of their students and also have certain clerical functions such as taking attendance, keeping other records, collecting lunch money, and keeping track of supplies.

As a result of these roles, certain *expectations* are held for the persons who fill them. For example, parents might expect the teacher to improve their child's reading and math skills, to improve the child's manners, or to work with them on the child's behavior problems. Teachers might expect the principal to handle difficult discipline problems, to hire teachers, to purchase supplies for the school, to assign students to classes, and to represent them to parents. The principal might expect the teachers to follow certain prescribed procedures for grading, to confer with parents about student progress, to assist with playground supervision, or to cover specific curriculum materials because of district requirements.

Unfortunately, these expectations do not always take into account the people who fill the roles. There is, therefore, a second dimension of the Getzels model, the *individual dimension,* which includes such things as how highly motivated people are, what values people in the system hold, or how independent or dependent members of the system are. This dimension accounts for the differences in people who occupy specific roles in the school. Each individual is a unique personality with differing physical, social, ego, and creative *needs*.[2] Some teachers may be perfectly comfortable with the principal who tells them what material they must cover; others may find little satisfaction in such a role. Some principals fit easily into an authoritarian role; others prefer to share responsibility.

Conflict between role definitions and individual needs sometimes can be useful in bringing about change in a school, because dissatisfaction may encourage people to look for new ways of doing things and new role definitions and may provide a good starting point for the change agent. However, it is more likely that deep-seated or extensive role conflict will absorb everyone's energy and impede meaningful change. The first step in creating conditions conducive to change in schools may be to create a climate where the institutional goals of the school and the individual needs of the people who work in the school are more compatible or can be made so.[3]

Research has suggested that an "open" climate is more likely to promote integration between the accomplishment of organizational purposes and the meeting of individual needs. In such a climate the members of the organization enjoy extremely high morale. The teachers are not burdened with mountains of busy work or by routine reports, and the principal's policies facilitate the teachers' accomplishment of their tasks. The teachers obtain considerable job satisfaction and are sufficiently motivated to overcome difficulties and frustrations. They have the incentive to work things out and to keep the organization moving. Furthermore, the teachers are proud to be associated with the school. Socially, the group members enjoy friendly relations with each other, but they apparently feel no need for an extremely high degree of intimacy. They are able to work together without bickering and griping.

This description of an open climate comes from the work of Halpin and Croft and serves as the basis for the Organizational Climate Description Questionnaire (OCDQ) that they developed.[4] The questionnaire is available to those who wish to measure the climate of their own school as a first step in planning change. It is necessary to recognize the existence of conflict or unproductive conditions before a start can be made toward changing them.

When there is conflict between the needs of individuals and the goals of systems, some form of adaptation takes place. Argyris, who conducted extensive research on organizations, has characterized four modes of adaptation: (1) leaving the organization, (2) moving to a higher position, (3) adopting defense mechanisms, or (4) turning apathetic and losing interest.[5] Almost every school has people whose actions fit these descriptions. There are teachers who leave because they disagree with the goals or structures to which they must subscribe. Some teachers become district office personnel or principals because they wish to change goals or structures, and other teachers or principals become defensive or apathetic because they feel "beaten down" by the system.

One reason why change is so difficult to bring about is that it often involves modifications in traditional roles. Since most people in the system have resolved the conflict between their needs and the demands of their role in some way which is comfortable for them, they will find changes that might upset this equilibrium threatening. The teacher who has decided that it is not worth fighting the system and has become apathetic may resist changes which require his active involvement and commitment. The person who has become a principal out of the desire to see things done "her way" may block changes calling for participatory decision making. Both have created comfortable roles for themselves and will resist situations which require them to search out and define new roles.[6]

Most changes which are now being suggested for schools involve such threats to traditional roles. New patterns of staffing are one example. The change from the self-contained classroom to team teaching or to differentiated staffing in which the teaching staff is made up of a hierarchy of teachers with differing skills will require teachers to rethink their roles and adapt to an entirely new set of expectations. Unless the problem is recognized and some provision is made which takes into account the problem of adapting to new roles, such changes are doomed to failure.

Processes

Expectations are met and roles are carried out within a set of organizational processes. Those interested in bringing about change in schools will be most successful if they concern themselves with such processes.

For our purposes, here, we shall look carefully at three of these: communication, decision making, and conflict management.

In its simplest form, *communication* involves a sender, a receiver, and a message. In successful communication, each of these elements will exhibit certain characteristics. First, the sender must have clearly in mind what he intends to achieve through his message. This means both that he must understand the factual data to be communicated and that he must be able to calculate the impact of the message upon those to whom it is directed. Second, a message must be stated in language which is comprehended similarly by sender and receiver. Vocabulary is tricky, and the same words do not mean the same thing to all people in all situations. Finally, the receiver must be ready and willing to hear and internalize what is being communicated.

The possibilities for breakdown in a communication system are considerable even under the best of circumstances. Perceptions and attitudes are involved; distortions occur. However, experience and research provide some principles to follow in improving communication in a school.

1   Information dispensed in the form of a written decree is generally less well received and understood than information dispensed in a face-to-face, two-way situation where questions can be asked and feedback gained. A principal, for example, is better off determining for whom his message is intended, seeking those people out, talking with them, and assuring himself of their understanding. Of course, brief announcements meant for a total staff can still be relegated to a memorandum so that they do not take up precious staff meeting time.

2   Insufficient information increases ambiguity and causes people to seek additional data from possibly unreliable sources. To avoid such a problem, one who communicates a message should constantly check perceptions to make sure that enough information is given and the correct meaning understood.

3   Information being dispensed through several levels of an organization may be distorted in the process. Thus, a superintendent who wishes to send a districtwide message should develop means to check with district officials, principals, teachers, and parents to assure that perceptions of meaning are in line with the intended meaning. Similarly, a principal or teacher should check with those who receive his messages.

4   Greater care must be given to the communication process when information that may be threatening is being communicated. Thus, messages about layoffs, cutbacks, transfers of personnel or resources,

and the like should be transmitted in a face-to-face mode or should be phrased with great care and perceptions of meaning spot-checked.

5 People tend to cooperate more fully if intended goals and outcomes have been mutually determined and adequately communicated. Constant discussion of purposes should be carried out between and among persons from all levels of a school and a school district. "Needs assessment" procedures, if conducted just once and then forgotten, can delude us into believing that the matter of purposes has been decided. The fact is, that as needs change, purposes do also. A constant dialogue is necessary.

6 The communication process is at its best when it is open and free, based upon mutual trust, with messages originating from and being sent to all parts of the school or school system. Trust takes time to build and it is only built through people demonstrating that they listen, hear what others say, respond, act upon what others say, and also behave as they say they will. Checking on how people feel about what is being said is a good technique for building openness in an organization such as a school.

7 Consistency and believability in communication efforts increase the chances of a message being heard. These qualities, closely related to trust, depend upon messages being sent in the same manner over time. They do not vacillate between being dictatorial and conciliatory or between being open and guarded. Further, the content of messages is substantiated by fact, past experience, or research.

Those interested in change should assess communication processes in the schools where they work. Further, if such processes seem to be malfunctioning and thus impeding the accomplishment of organizational expectations, corrective action should be taken in the form of altering structures or by providing communication training.[7]

One of the most critical processes in any organization is *decision making*. This is particularly true today when both community groups and teachers are calling for more involvement in the education process and when everyone seems to be suggesting some form of decentralization. However, for the most part, the question still remains: "Who shall make what decision for and in the schools?" Many schools and school districts are working on answers to this critical question. There are school advisory councils, school district management teams involving representatives of many groups, school planning councils which involve teachers in schoolwide decision making, citizen advisory groups to advise boards of education, and many other structures aimed at broad involvement.

One thing we know is that we can no longer rely on decisions made only by those designated as "leaders" or administrators. Just as the President alone is not going to save the nation from recession, energy shortages, pollution, or inflation, neither is the principal alone going to save the school from low achievement, poor instruction, overcrowded classes, or campus violence. The administrator who controls all decisions is limiting the creativity of others while at the same time creating a bottleneck which often frustrates needed immediate action. Also, we know that decisions need to be as close as possible to their consequences. Thus, decisions about the classroom need to be made by teachers and those with whom they work. Decisions about the school budget need to be made by a group representative of the total school population.

There are techniques which can be used to clarify decision making in schools and school districts. For example, at the school-district level, groups can be called together which represent "role-alike" people (e.g., board members in a group, superintendents in a group, representative teachers in a group, representative advisory council members in a group) to define their decision-making roles with regard to such matters as budget, personnel, and instruction. At a later date these results can be submitted to groups which represent all roles. These groups can then take the results of the earlier "role-alike" activity and determine or negotiate districtwide and school-level decision-making roles. Through such a procedure all groups are represented in the determination of decision-making processes.[8]

Finally, clarifying decision-making roles is a necessary prerequisite to assigning accountability. Presently, in American education, the pervasive movement to accountability appears to be focusing upon the teacher or at best the local school. The fact is that teachers cannot be held accountable for decisions made by others in the educational hierarchy, particularly when the origin of so many decisions is hidden in a bureaucratic maze. The result of applying pressure on teachers for more accountability without giving them parallel freedom over decisions which affect their daily work and without assigning accountability to others in the educational hierarchy for their decisions can only result in heightened efforts on the part of teachers to protect themselves through strong associations and unions. The ultimate outcome then will be the removal of the decision-making process from the school. Chapter 4 will discuss more fully where the responsibility for various types of decisions should lie.

The third critical process in schools is *conflict management*. It is closely related to communication in that conflict is often heightened in situations where disagreeing parties do not communicate with each other frequently and openly. Likewise, conflict frequently arises from struggles for decision-making authority over the allocation of resources, the determination of organizational goals and policies, the determination of means to be employed to reach organizational goals, or the selection and deployment of personnel. Thus, the improvement of communication structures and the clarification of decision-making roles in schools can do much to head off unnecessary conflict.

There are many factors involved in organizational conflicts. For example, individual needs, desires, and motives (promotion, recognition, job security) can often cause conflict (e.g., two teachers vying for a department chairmanship). Even more important, organization members frequently hold different value positions and philosophies of life and education. To be managed, conflicts over ideas need to be brought out into the open. Further, such conflicts can often be resolved through the identification of areas of common accord among those in disagreement. For example, in a case where teachers disagree over methods of teaching reading, a good place to begin would be to identify those skills they can all agree upon as being important to be taught and learned. It should be remembered, though, that conflict resolution should involve as many of the conflicting parties and interests as possible, even though some parties at times seem to be unreasonable or obstructionist.

Where conflicts develop, it is important that the overriding goals of the organization predominate over the narrower goals of particular vested-interest groups. However, solutions to conflicts cannot be imposed, even if the solutions seem to be in line with organizational goals. While imposed solutions may seem to smooth over an immediate conflict situation, they often create hostilities which later serve as the basis for additional and often more serious conflicts. If, as was suggested earlier, there has been frequent and broad-based discussion of and agreement upon purposes, there will be little need for those in a school to rely upon authority figures to resolve conflicts which involve the basic goals of schooling.

With the advent of many categorical programs (early childhood education, bilingual education, Right-to-Read), many schools will employ additional people and there will be much more differentiation in roles. Thus, some people will become "staff." That is, they will be employed to serve teachers as consultants or helpers. While, in the main, these people will improve the educational program of the school, it should be recognized that their presence adds to the potential for conflict. It is natural for people employed in "staff" positions to justify their existence, seek acceptance of their contributions, and build "line" dependence upon their work. But it must be remembered that the function of "staff" people, such as consultants, is to apply their specialized knowledge in problem areas and to advise those in "line" positions. Principals and teachers must make the final decisions and be held accountable for them.

Finally, school people, who sometimes tend to be conciliatory by nature, need to recognize that conflict is not necessarily a bad thing. It can cause tensions which, if dealt with openly, can result in more precision in goals, better methods of instruction, fuller utilization of resources, and improved outcomes of schooling—the "stuff" of change.

Informal Norms

The fourth dimension of the social system of the school, the *informal dimension,* has to do with processes which are "extralegal"—that is, not formally sanctioned or institutionalized by the governing apparatus. Such informal relationships among members of the system often serve to acomplish goals more effectively than the functional role relationships of the formal system. A principal, for example, who wishes to get alterations in his building to facilitate team teaching may do better by discussing the matter at a social event with the appropriate district administrator than by sending formal requests through regular channels. Similarly, opinion leaders among teachers often hold the key to where, when, and what changes can be made in the school. It is these opinion leaders and the informal groups to which they belong who often set the norms for or against change in a school. Ianaccone suggests that a conscious effort should be made to build interaction between formal and informal power stuctures within the school through the development of open communication, information flow, and formal participatory decision making so that the formal goals of the institution and the informal norms of the group can be meshed together as closely as possible.[9]

Organizational Complexity

Any discussion of change in schools must also recognize a fifth dimension of school life, the fact that schools vary markedly in terms of their *organizational complexity.* Brief descriptions of two elementary schools provide an example.

The first school serves a rather stable middle-income community and has a pupil enrollment of approximately 600. A principal and twenty teachers make up the professional staff. Secretarial, custodial, and cafeteria staff number eight, and support personnel such as speech therapists and psychometrists are on call. Teachers are aided by six paid paraprofessionals and numerous volunteer aids. The financial support for the school is based upon a $900 per year figure per student ($540,000), of which approximately 20 percent is administered at the building level. The local PTA and community advisory council are active and supportive of the school program. Pupil achievement-test scores, by and large, are above local, state, and national norms.

The second school serves a mobile population made up of different racial and ethnic groups. Pupils are mainly from low-income families. Enrollment ranges from 1500 to 1550 students, depending upon the time of year. A principal, two vice-principals, a counselor, and various support personnel are housed in the building. There are an office manager, four secretaries, six custodians, and ten cafeteria workers. Fifty-one regular classroom teachers are aided by twenty paid paraprofessionals and numerous volunteers. The regular financial support is based upon the $900 per year figure per student ($1,372,500) of which approximately 20 percent is administered at the building level. However, there is an additional $1,000,000 being administered at the building level for five special programs including Title I-ESEA for disadvantaged students, early childhood education, a preschool program, a free breakfast program, and a community tutorial program. Those who administer the programs are responsible to school district and state officials and in one case to a private foundation. Because of these special programs there are some twelve professional staff members who serve in various capacities as resource people for teachers. The local PTA and community advisory council are relatively inactive except for a few quite vocal members who have affiliations with various groups in the community. Pupil achivement test scores, in the main, are below local, state, and national norms.

It becomes obvious from the brief descriptions of these two elementary schools (not to mention large secondary schools) that schools differ widely in their organizational complexity. We feel that examining and understanding the school's complexity can contribute greatly to managing the problems of change. For example, while norms and roles may be well defined in the smaller school, there could be problems of resistance to change because of a certain amount of satisfaction with the status quo. On the other hand, while there may be a desire to change in the second school, bureaucratic structures, unclear norms and roles, or problems of communication could impede change efforts.

Hage and Aiken have worked on analyzing change in complex social organizations such as schools and have developed a series of hypotheses about change in these organizations based on the following definitions:[10]

Program change—the addition, deletion, or alteration of a service or product designed to meet a new goal or to better reach an established goal

Complexity—the level of knowledge and expertise in an organization

Centralization—the way in which power is distributed in an organization

Formalization—the degree of codification of jobs in an organization

Stratification—the differential distribution of rewards to the jobs in an organization

Production (achievement)—the relative emphasis on the quantity or quality of the organization's products or services

Efficiency—the relative emphasis on the cost reduction of the product or service

Job satisfaction—the degree of morale among the job occupants in the organization

Here are some of the hypotheses proposed by Hage and Aiken with illustrative examples from schools:

1 The greater the rate of complexity, the greater the rate of program change (teachers who have many opportunities for in-service training will create a variety of new program options for students)

2 The higher the centralization, the lower the rate of program change (when teachers have to seek administrative approval for program changes they will seek fewer such changes)

3 The greater the formalization, the lower the rate of program change (in schools where there is a high degree of formal specialization among staff members or with categorical programs or departmentalization, there will be fewer efforts to create program changes)

4 The greater the stratification, the lower the rate of program change (when higher salaries are paid to people for specialized roles in a school such as team leader, curriculum specialist, reading specialist, and counselor, there will be fewer efforts to create program changes)

5 The higher the volume of production, the lower the rate of program change (in schools where achievement test scores are high, there will be fewer efforts to change programs)

6 The greater the emphasis on efficiency, the lower the rate of program change (where efforts are made to conserve money by doing such things as raising class size or making teachers more accountable, there will be fewer program changes)

7 The higher the job satisfaction, the greater the rate of program change (when teachers feel motivated, appreciated, and trusted, they will, in turn, create a variety of new program options for students)

If such hypotheses prove to be true, they would lead to some dramatic conclusions about how schools and school districts should be reorganized. Highly trained staff members would be desirable. Decision making would be decentralized. Role distinctions would be minimized. Adult-pupil ratios would be reduced. Emphasis on efficiency or accountability would be minimized. Morale and motivation of professionals and students would become paramount. Perhaps those of us concerned with change in schools have at least a partial agenda to be tested.

EXTERNAL RELATIONSHIPS

Any open system is in constant interaction with its environment. Individuals and groups in that environment constantly make demands upon the system or provide it with supports. Such demands and supports are referred to as *inputs*. A vote for a school bond or tax issue is an input, in this case a support input. Likewise, a demand from an individual or a group for an improved reading program is an input. Generally, such inputs are made to the system from one of four sources: individuals, associational groups, nonassociational groups, or anomic groups.[11]

Associational groups are well organized and tend to represent special interests over a long period of time. They have well-organized means of presenting their demands: lobbying, use of media, legal expertise, and so forth. Taxpayers' associations, religious groups, organized conservation groups, the John Birch Society, and the National Association for the Advancement of Colored People (NAACP) are all examples of associational groups, and their numbers are growing. One study of the Los Angeles City Unified School District showed that there were some thirteen different types of organized groups which presented nearly 2,000 demands to the board of education during one school year.[12] These groups continually campaign for or against school issues in line with their own interests. Accountability in the use of school monies, prayer in schools, ecological curricula, basic education, black history, and sex education are issues which associational groups might favor or oppose. While such groups tend to concentrate at state or school district levels, they frequently can be found active at the local school level, particularly when it will serve their larger interests. More importantly, because of the ability of such groups to make their views known through the news media, they are effective in causing local public opinion to coalesce. Practitioners must be aware of such forces and, in addition, recognize that they can be enlisted in efforts to bring about changes in schooling.

Nonassociational groups are those which tend to organize around specific issues, work for or against these issues, and then disband as groups. A group which forms to get a stoplight installed at a school crosswalk where there is heavy traffic or a group formed to effect the firing of a teacher is a nonassociational group. Such groups do tend to concentrate their efforts at the local school level. Occasionally, such groups will form temporary linkages with larger, more powerful associational groups. Again, practitioners must be aware of such groups and must be willing to work with them or at least deal with them.

During the sixties, a new input phenomenon appeared on the school scene, the formation of *anomic groups*. Such groups tend to organize spontaneously, to focus at the local school level, and to use violent means to put forth their demands. Sit-ins, riots, burnings, and pickets are anomic occurrences which frequently have brought about changes in schooling. Generally, anomic groups arise out of frustration or perceived disenfranchisement. When people outside the system (or inside, for that matter) resort to anomic means to make their wishes known, it is usually symptomatic of the fact that, for one reason or another, they see normal channels of demand articulation closed to them. Practitioners should examine such channels and such perceptions carefully and should attempt to keep channels of communication open.

Since the 1950s, critics of the schools have been multiplying from both the right and the left. The right wing was the first to be heard from with its sympathizers viewing the federal government's involvement with schooling as a threat to individual liberty and discovering a "communist plot" in many proposed new curricula or methods,[13] such as sex education, "look-say" methods of teaching reading, the new math, or assigned reading of novels such as *The Catcher in the Rye*. The left was not far behind with the advent of community action groups and poor and minority groups who attacked what they saw as conservative school programs which were unresponsive to the needs of large segments of the population. While the small and vocal right was often able to close down programs like sex education, the changes called for by the left—bussing, affirmative action, or minority studies— usually polarized the community and led to stalemate or even violence. Unfortunately, as a result of the activities of both sides, school people have become less willing to explore changes which appear to have any potential for creating controversy. The "don't-rock-the-boat" syndrome is more common than perhaps most educators would like to admit, particularly in times when the school job market is down and mobility is lessened.

The critical point is that schools as open systems *interact* with the rest of society. This seems such an obvious statement that many would question that it needs to be made. However, the fact is that many schools and school districts often behave institutionally as if such interaction does not exist. More often than not, they react to rather than interact with the society they serve. Tax elections serve as a perfect example. From the end of World War II until the early or mid-sixties, school districts across the nation almost annually went to their voters with new tax or bond elections. By and large, such elections were successful, and both operating and building funds were readily available to the schools. Such tax issues became so common during that period that administrative training programs began to include courses in "public relations," which were clearly directed at training people to plan and win tax elections. Similarly, school districts often employed full-time staffs or consultant firms to operate such elections. Almost every school principal who served during those years can remember vividly his efforts to organize his PTA or other parent groups for the annual or biannual tax election. Many teachers can recall campaigning from house to house.

There are many reasons why more and more tax elections and bond issues have been defeated since the mid-sixties; war, inflation, inadequate tax structures, and competition for tax dollars are only some examples. There is another, perhaps more significant reason, however. Given all the conditions mentioned above, the defeat of tax elections can also be attributed to the manner in which school people approach the voters for support.

To begin with, school people frequently are defensive and somewhat secretive about what they do inside the walls of the school. They resist, in great measure, the involvement of parents and other community members in the "professional" affairs of the school. Aside from "back-to-school" nights, open houses, PTA meetings, and occasional parent-teacher conferences, parents are typically contacted only when a student has misbehaved in some way or when there is a tax or bond election. More often than not, the questioning parent has been looked upon as meddlesome or even as a troublemaker. Even with the recent advent of community advisory councils at local schools, the defensive and distrustful attitude of school people toward parents is still too much in evidence. A sense of mutual trust and respect cannot be built between school and community when the school seems closed and the community is called upon only in time of financial need.

Second, tax election campaigns often have been carried on with real problems glossed over. Voters are approached with the notion that "our schools are doing great and we need more money to keep up the good work." However, such reasoning somehow escapes the taxpayer, who sees low standardized-achievement-test scores published in the local newspaper or who sees his child's special needs not being met by the school. It seems obvious that voters will not respond to tax elections unless they know what the real problems of schooling are.

Finally, and probably out of desperation, many school districts, particularly after losing several tax elections, have resorted to threatening the community with drastic measures. These threats include such things as going on double sessions, dropping the athletic program, curtailing the music program, cutting off one period for high school students, eliminating counselors and nurses, raising class size, or closing schools early if tax or bond elections are not passed. Generally speaking, people do not like to be threatened. Also, many taxpayers do not believe that school people have the right to cut in sensitive areas such as athletics, counseling, or health services. In many cases, school districts repeatedly make such threats and then ultimately work out ways to continue or restore threatened cuts. In so doing, they create a disbelieving public which ultimately reacts sluggishly or even negatively when real cuts are necessary. Chapter 5 will deal more fully with the problem of taxation and school finance.

A final example of the reactive nature of schools to demands from outside the school has to do with those classified as anomic or violent. While such demands have frequently arisen out of frustration or a feeling of disenfranchisement on the part of some individual or group, too frequently the school has failed to deal with or even examine the root causes of such frustration. Often, some form of repressive action is taken. Many urban high schools have become veritable prisons with high fences and a proliferation of "security" guards, rather than centers of community problem solving wherein the root causes of violence are identified and dealt with.

IMPLICATIONS

The discussion in this chapter suggests that change in the school is a difficult thing to bring about. A systemic view, however, gives those who are interested in such change indications of where they can begin or with what they must deal. There are different types of groups making demands and providing supports to schools. Some are well organized and have special interests. Others are less well organized and have only specific, temporary interests. Practitioners can and should interact with those outside the school and should go so far as to assist in organizing specific groups in the name of change rather than merely being reactive to pressures brought to bear on them from outside the school.

Internally, the school is a composite of goals or expectations, personal needs, group norms, and sensitive processes. They are in constant interaction and cannot be treated independently by change agents. Anyone who wishes to change the goals of a school must at the same time be willing to invest time in changing norms and processes which might impede goal accomplishment. Also, he must be alert to how the new goals relate to personal needs of staff members. An open climate, with its participatory modes of decision making, most often allows for successful integration of goals, needs, and norms. Creation of such a climate might be the first focus of the change agent's efforts.

Finally, schools have the characteristics of all complex organizations to one degree or another. Research into such organizations suggests that the areas which offer the most potential for improving schools are those which involve training staff, decentralizing decision making, minimizing role distinctions, improving staff morale, and the like.

Recognizing the complexity of schools and designing change strategies which deal with these complexities is a logical first step in planning change. In a sense, it represents a "scientific" or analytic approach. Unfortunately, there are a whole set of circumstances which shape up as further obstacles to change. These are presented by the sociopolitical context of the school, which will be considered in the next chapter.

NOTES

1   For an application of the Getzels model to the analysis of change in actual school settings see Richard C. Williams, Charles C. Wall, W. Michael Martin, and Arthur Berchin, *Effecting Organizational Renewal in Schools: A Social Systems Perspective*, McGraw-Hill, New York, 1974.

2   A helpful way of viewing man's needs is put forth in Abraham Maslow, "A Theory of Human Motivation," *Psychological Review*, vol. 50, pp. 370–396, 1943. Maslow suggests that man is a wanting animal —as soon as one need is satisfied, another appears in its place. Further, he sees man moving through the satisfaction of a hierarchy of individual needs: physiological, social, ego, self-fulfillment. For an application of this concept to schools see chap. 2 in John I. Goodlad, M. Frances Klein, Jerrold M. Novotney, Kenneth A. Tye, and Associates, *Toward a Mankind School: An Adventure in Humanistic Education*, McGraw-Hill, New York, 1974.

3   A study of eight elementary schools has shown that schools which rate high in ability to achieve their goals have less role conflict than those which are rated low. See Williams, Wall, Martin, and Berchin, op. cit., chap. 3.

4   Andrew W. Halpin and Don B. Croft, *The Organizational Climate of Schools*, U.S. Office of Education, Washington, D.C., 1962, p. 80.

5   Chris Argyris, *Personality and Organization: The Conflict between System and the Individual*, Harper & Row, New York, 1957.

6   Changing role expectations can cause serious role conflicts for individuals in the school and among various groups with differing expectations. For an in-depth but practical discussion of role conflict for the principal in a changing school, see Mary M. Bentzen, "Conflicting Roles," in Jerrold M. Novotney (ed.), *The Principal and the Challenge of Change*, Institute for Development of Educational Activities, Inc., monograph, Melbourne, Fla., 1968.

7   There are good training programs for school people, for example, the one developed by the Northwest Regional Educational Laboratory. See Charles Jung et al., *Interpersonal Communication*, Xicon, Inc., Sterling Forest, N.Y., 1972.

8   Such a procedure was successfully designed and implemented in La Cañada Unified School District in Southern California under the direction of Dr. Donald Ziehl, Superintendent.

9   Laurence Ianaccone, "An Approach to the Informal Organization of the School," in Daniel E. Griffiths (ed.), *Behavioral Science and Educational Administration*, National Society for the Study of Education, Sixty-third Yearbook, Part II, The University of Chicago Press, Chicago, 1964, chap. X, pp. 223–242.

10   Jerald Hage and Michael Aiken, *Social Change in Complex Organizations*, Random House, New York, 1970.

11   These categories are derived from the works of the political scientist Gabriel Almond. See his "A Functional Approach to Comparative Politics," in Gabriel A. Almond and James S. Coleman (eds.), *The Politics of the Developing Areas*, Princeton, Princeton, N.J., 1960, pp. 3–64.

12   Kenneth A. Tye, "A Conceptual Framework for Political Analysis, Public Demands and School Board Decisions," unpublished doctoral dissertation, University of California, Los Angeles, 1968, pp. 136–138.

13   Mary Anne Raywid, *The Ax-Grinders*, Macmillan, New York, 1962.

CHAPTER 4

THE SOCIOPOLITICAL CONTEXT OF SCHOOLING

In 1962, the California Legislature mandated that all sixth, seventh, and eighth grade students in the state, exclusive of the mentally retarded, were to receive foreign-language instruction. The legislation was not based on a need identified by research, for at the time research on foreign-language instruction had not shown that any great benefit was gained by moving foreign-language instruction downward to the elementary school level, and it certainly had not shown that all students should study a foreign language.[1] At best, the legislature's action could be excused as a reaction to a perceived Soviet educational superiority resulting from the launching of Sputnik in 1957. At worst, the votes were there because foreign languages had become fashionable.

From the educator's point of view, it was an irresponsible act which created havoc in the schools of California. More irresponsible still, no funds were allocated for carrying out such a sweeping mandate. Only National Defense Education Act (NDEA) funds were available, and they were granted on a project-by-project approval basis by the state department of education.

The elementary schools of the state were totally unprepared to add foreign languages to their curricula. However, forced to comply with the legislation, schools and school districts responded as best they could. Projects were written for NDEA funds. "Teacher-free" materials, many of them excellent and many of them not, were purchased. Coordinators and consultants were employed. Foreign-language teachers were employed or trained. Syllabi were written. Educational television was brought into play. Class schedules were developed or redeveloped.

Though many good programs were designed and implemented in schools throughout the state, the ultimate results were negative on at least two counts. First, much bad instruction took place. For example, hundreds of youngsters were herded into auditoriums and "exposed" to television broadcasts without adequate classroom follow-up. Second, because each school or district designed its own program, the problems of articulation between elementary and secondary programs became confused, to say the least.

The fallacy of this legislation became clearer and clearer as the target year (1965) for statewide implementation approached. Countless exclusions were granted to school districts throughout the state which were unable to meet the deadline. By 1968, the legislation had been rewritten to the effect that beginning with the seventh grade foreign languages were to be offered by schools to all students who wished to take them. And still no monies were allocated by the state for implementation of foreign-language instruction.

Stories like the one of foreign-language instruction in California are not unique. Other restrictive, directive, and categorical legislation has been and still is being passed by state legislatures throughout the nation. The point is not that foreign-language instruction is inappropriate at the elementary school level but that state legislatures often make inappropriate decisions which radically affect what schools can and should do. The problem is compounded further by the fact that other levels of the educational system likewise make such decisions. Thus, while we can view the school itself as an "open system," we must also remember that the school is a subsystem of the greater educational "open system" which includes the federal government, state governments, school boards, school districts, and other educational agencies. The practitioner in the school must understand this sociopolitical suprasystem, for what happens there affects dramatically what the school can and will do.

THE FEDERAL GOVERNMENT

Prior to the sixties, governmental roles in education were rather well defined in this nation. There was *local control* of education, there was *state responsibility* for education, and there was *federal concern* for education.[2] However, in 1954, this legal and cultural tradition began to change with the U.S. Supreme Court decision on Brown versus the Board of Education of Topeka, in which the nation was ordered to desegregate its schools.

In the 1960s, Congress assumed an activist role in education, passing the Economic Opportunity Act (EOA) in 1964. This legislation called for direct federal intervention in education through programs such as Job Corps for high school dropouts and Headstart for culturally disadvantaged preschool children. In 1965, the Elementary and Secondary Education Act (ESEA) was directed at the accomplishment of four goals: (1) improving the quality of education for economically and culturally disadvantaged children and youth of the nation, (2) encouraging innovation in the schools of the nation, (3) promoting educational research, and (4) upgrading state departments of education. Specific guidelines were drawn up by the U.S. Office of Education and rigorously applied to the disbursement of federal monies to local schools, school districts, and state and intermediate educational agencies.

ESEA also strengthened the Office of Education. Its functions had been primarily those of data gathering, disbursing and accounting for limited federal monies, and disseminating information.[3] Almost overnight, with the passage of ESEA, the federal role in American education changed radically. Instead of its historical *concern* for education, the federal government assumed *responsibility* for the accomplishment of specific national goals through the disbursement of categorical monies and through the establishment of guidelines which directed how such monies would be spent.

We do not know just how much responsibility or even control of education the federal government will eventually have. Some evidence suggests that an effort is being made to keep federal involvement in education to a minimum. For example, since 1967, more and more of the administration of federal programs has been turned over to state agencies. Also, while actual federal dollar support has risen slightly over the past several years, revenue for public elementary and secondary schools, as a percentage of total revenue, dropped each year from a high of 8.0 in fiscal 1968 to 6.9 in fiscal 1971.[4] Finally, the concept of revenue sharing can be viewed as a major step away from federal involvement in education. Carried to its ultimate, all federal monies for education would be returned to the states on some formula basis for the states to administer.

There are other signs that federal responsibility for education may grow in the years to come. Congress is still passing legislation which involves the federal government in more and more educational areas. The Education Professions Development Act provided over one billion dollars in 1967 for training programs for education personnel. The Public Broadcasting Act of 1967 created a public television corporation.

Programs in guidance, dropout prevention, bilingual education, and education of the handicapped have all been added to ESEA since 1965. The National Institute of Education (NIE) was formed at the federal level in 1972, separate from the Office of Education, to encourage massive research and development efforts in education.[5] There is continued discussion of raising education to a cabinet-level position in the federal government because, as only one office in the Department of Health, Education, and Welfare, education cannot get the hearing it really needs. Finally, discussions of revenue efforts such as a federal value-added tax to support education clearly indicate that federal responsibility may continue to grow.

At least six forces determine how the federal government will ultimately affect what goes on in the local school: (1) the President and his immediate advisors, (2) the Office of Education and other administrative agencies, (3) the Congress, (4) the education lobbies, (5) other vested interest groups, and (6) the courts.

The President determines the overall federal administrative stance toward public education. Lyndon Johnson, a former teacher, was so pro-education that he has often been referred to as the "Education President." On the other hand, Richard Nixon gave only tacit support to public education and, in fact; more than once vetoed or held up educational legislation which he termed inflationary.

The U.S. Office of Education (OE) administers programs established by the Congress, proposes legislation to the Congress, enforces court rulings, and carries out general administrative policies established by the president and his advisers. The U.S. Commissioner of Education is OE's chief officer. He is a political appointee and is in a potentially powerful position as the administration's chief advisor on education matters and as the chief administration representative to the Congress. As the federal role in education has expanded, so has the role of the Office of Education and the power of the commissioner. The expansion of OE has caused changes in countless schools across the country. As schools have accepted federal monies and guidelines, they have had to hire new and different kinds of personnel (e.g., bilingual teachers, subject specialists, teacher aides). They have had to search out new equipment and materials and reorganize space. They have had to provide in-service training for staff members. Frequently, they have had to involve community members in decision making. These are all changes which cause corresponding changes in structures, functions, norms, roles, processes, and informal networks in the social system of the school. Unfortunately, these changes are too infrequently attended to as schools respond to national priorities and accept federal funds and involvement in federal programs. It is for this reason that added funds alone often make no significant difference in terms of what really happens to students.

One of the realities of federal activity in education is that it involves several agencies, such as the Departments of Defense, Labor, and Interior, and many others which have education programs related to the ongoing activities of schools. High school ROTC programs and the Department of Labor Manpower Development programs are two examples. There are many who advocate that all education programs should be brought into one central agency and that that agency should be raised to the department level with cabinet representation. They feel that having all education programs in one department would allow for better articulation and eliminate overlap. Those who oppose a strong department of education tend to fear federal control and centralized decision making. They are strong advocates of local control.

Congress is charged with the responsibility of assessing the values, needs, and wants of society and passing laws which express those values or meet those needs and wants. Though legislation is generally drawn up by the executive branch, it is Congress which must pass it and authorize and allocate funds for its implementation. As the federal government takes on more of the burden of financing education, the level of funding available to schools will be dependent upon the workings of Congress. However, in Congress, education must vie with other welfare needs (medical care, transportation, social security) and defense needs for its share of the federal revenue.

The education lobby or "establishment" at the national level is made up of many organizations. The 1969 *Contact Washington* lists 105 organizations, associations, and councils located in Washington, D.C., which have direct interests in education.[6] This listing does not include the various departments, national affiliates, and associated organizations of the National Education Association. In addition, other interest groups which are not directly connected with education have an influence on educational policy, as Campbell and Layton describe the situation:

> The non-educational interest groups operating in Washington are numerous, and many of them strongly seek to influence educational policies. These groups include the U.S. Chamber of Commerce, the American

Farm Bureau, The AFL-CIO, and the United States Catholic Conference. We have also to consider the James B. Conants, the Jerrold Zachariases, the Hyman Rickovers, and the other highly respected educational proponents, critics, and experts. Some of them bring great prestige to their points of view and through Congress's esteem for them are able to promote certain educational policies effectively. While in the states professional associations and interest groups sometimes play roles in policy formulation, even to the extent of having legislation drafted in their offices, they are less likely to play similar roles at the national level. It seems that their contributions at the national level are primarily of a negative nature; they can alter and even veto legislation and policies they do not want, but they seldom are able to initiate policies.[7]

Finally, at the federal level, the courts have increased their influence over what happens in education, particularly in the area of integration. Beginning with the 1954 decision, the courts have continually required school districts to design plans for desegregating schools. Some decisions have called specifically for bussing, while in other cases redistricting or "open" attendance plans drafted by school districts have been acceptable to the courts. The recent court decisions against cross-district bussing appear to be a setback for the advocates of integration. However, just how far the courts ultimately will go in the matter of desegregation is not now clear.

Court decisions regarding desegregation can have dramatic effects upon schools. Where whole student bodies change, student needs are different, different programs are needed, teaching techniques must be altered, and personnel has to be changed. Higher or lower levels of funding can cause changes in programs and personnel, also.

Changes in schools will come about as a result of other issues being dealt with by the courts. Privacy rights with regard to record keeping, entrance and personnel quotas, and support for parochial schools are all issues yet to be decided finally. In these instances and in others yet to come, court decisions, without doubt, will cause dramatic changes in the school social system. Again, it is the system variables which must be dealt with if the school is to be effective as it sets about to change as a result of direct or indirect actions at the federal level.

Perhaps the one remaining argument, as yet unresolved, concerning federal involvement in education is whether it should be general or categorical.[8] One position is that the federal government should support public education through block grants-in-aid to states. The compelling arguments for this position are that such grants can be sustaining, that they provide for an ongoing vitality of state and local governments, and that they do not usurp the decision-making power of these levels. The opposing position is that federal monies should be expended to support national priorities such as equality of educational opportunity and quality educational programs for all. Proponents of this position argue that state agencies are weak and ineffective, that general aid allows local biases to supplant national priorities, and that urban areas where educational needs are the greatest would be the losers without direct federal intervention.

The manner in which the general-categorical issue is resolved in the years to come will have serious implications for the practitioner and for the single school unit. For example, if the final resolution of the argument were to fall on the general-aid side, one could envision the neighborhood school concept lasting into the twenty-first century. On the other hand, if the categorical argument were to win out, one could envision new school district configurations with much more urban-suburban collaboration. The result might be open attendance with schools specializing in alternative programs. Resolution of the question needs to be pursued actively. To date, educators, when not protecting their own vested interests, have tended to leave the question to the politicians and the courts to decide for them.

THE STATE

Historically, public education in the United States has been defined as a state responsibility. Although school programs throughout the country bear remarkable similarities to each other, the manner in which the state influences schooling varies greatly from state to state.

In general, the state legislature is the most influential body at the state level, since it establishes the broad policy guidelines for educational programs. Most state legislatures are actively involved in educational matters. A review of the activities of state legislatures throughout the nation shows that they are deeply involved in making educational decisions about such things as curriculum, instruction, finance, construction, and accountability that affect the daily lives of those in the schools.[9]

In addition to the state legislature, at least six other state agencies and groups affect what goes on in the local school: (1) the governor and his advisers, (2) the state board of education, (3) the state department of education, (4) the education lobbies, (5) other vested interest groups, and (6) the state courts.

Issues such as school integration and means of financing education more and more are occupying the daily news; consequently, politicians are increasingly concerned with such issues. Governors are beginning to take very active roles in educational policy formation, at times sharing such roles with legislatures.

Nearly all states have state boards of education which have responsibility for the supervision of elementary and secondary education and for operationalizing the general directives of the legislature. In some cases board members are elected; in others they are appointed by the governor. State boards oversee state departments of education, which administer the educational policies formulated by the legislatures and boards. Often the state departments, particularly their chief officers, play a strong role in recommending legislation or board action.

As at the federal level, lobbies for or against various educational propositions are active at the state level. Campbell and Layton describe these interest groups as follows:

> There are many educational organizations which may play vigorous policy roles. The most important of these organizations are usually the state teachers' association, the state school administrators' organization, the state school boards' association, the state Parent Teachers Association. In many state capitals, there are also representatives of teacher unions who are active in attempting to influence policy. There are many other private associations whose interests are not exclusively tied to education but who become involved in educational decisions. State chambers of commerce, taxpayers' groups, AFL-CIO affiliates, and agricultural associations are examples. The interest groups seldom initiate policies, but they often are able to alter or veto potential changes in policy. In addition, there are always knowledgeable persons, particularly in business and the professions, who as individuals make their impact on particular policies.[10]

State courts, like their federal counterparts, influence schooling in significant ways. Of particular note are the decisions in California, Michigan, New Jersey, and Texas, among others, which in one way or another questioned the local property tax as a viable means of providing major financial support for public education. The ultimate outcome of such decisions will have great import for schools since they imply less money for some schools and more money for others.

In considering the state responsibility for education, particular attention has to be directed to the changing relationships between the states and urban school districts. This changing relationship was initiated by the federal legislation of the mid and late sixties which recognized that by 1980 some 80 percent of all school-age children would be enrolled in urban areas[11] and which further recognized that the poor and minorities who lived in urban areas did not have educational opportunities equal to those of their suburban brothers and sisters. It was reinforced by the "one man, one vote" ruling of the U.S. Supreme Court in 1964 which was directed at breaking down the rural domination of American political processes. Finally, state court rulings against the property tax are another factor in creating a new state-urban relationship which includes increased funding for urban schools. Along with the funds go guidelines for establishing programs and direct monitoring and evaluation of school programs by state agency personnel. In many instances, spurred on by decentralization efforts in large city school districts, the practical result is a direct state-to-school line of communications, one which frequently circumvents or ignores in great measure the local school district officials and the local school board. In the school itself, the result can be a dramatic increase in paper work and required reporting.

Interestingly, many state officials have decried federal involvement in education, much of which has been directed toward urban problems. This attitude, combined with programs causing federal monies to flow through the states (e.g., the Quie Amendment and Revenue sharing), means that state officials will have to take on the problem of equalizing educational opportunity and providing for quality education for all children. Whether or not state governments are capable of or seriously dedicated to meeting these responsibilities may well be the educational drama of the next decade, a drama which educators should watch carefully or, even better, in which they should actively participate. Advocates of local control, who formerly decried federal control, are now beginning to see the specter of state control.[12]

THE LOCAL LEVEL

The local governance of schooling is quite different from district to district. There are dependent districts which are subunits of city govern-

ments, total county units as in Maryland and Florida, districts contain-
ing both secondary and elementary schools, and separate elementary
and secondary school districts which have overlapping boundaries.
Despite these differences, however, surveys have shown that programs
in schools, by and large, are marked by sameness.[13]

Legally, state responsibility is extended from the state to local
boards of education which are responsible for the establishment of
policies, the conversion of policies into rules of operation, and the application of policies and rules to specific cases which come before
them. Such policy and rule making and application are carried out in
a variety of areas—finance, personnel, curriculum, materials of instruction, facilities, and so forth. Typically, when the community wishes a
change in schooling or when the members of a community wish to
resist a change, their demands are focused upon the local school
board. Likewise, teacher demands are focused at the local board level.

As discussed in Chapter 3, the frequency and number of demands
upon local school boards have increased over the past decade. Such
activity has also led to increased political activity surrounding boards,
including recall elections to replace board members. Such a phenomenon is understandable when one considers both the generally increased
interest in education and the general feeling of frustration with national and state politics. The involvement of the United States in Indochina, inflation, higher taxes, and a generally depressed economy have
made the public more conscious of all government expenditures.
While the public feels that it can do little about national issues, it
knows that it has a measure of control over education. Thus, it has become eager to exercise this control by becoming involved with such
issues as bussing and school finance.

While such involvement is a healthy sign, it also can be troublesome. First, particularly in large districts, local boards of education are
not as responsive to community demands as they should be.[14] Second,
many demands made upon local school boards cannot be dealt with
by the boards because, in reality, they are matters which various
state or even federal agencies must resolve. The issue of finance is a
good example. As much as boards might wish to deal with financial
issues, they often have little control over large portions of their budget
while their means of producing revenues have been restricted, and so
they have to wait until complicated issues are hammered out at the
state or federal level.

Besides the school board, there are many other individuals and groups that play important roles in local decision making at the school district level. For example, there are the professionals—the superintendent, district administrators, supervisors, and coordinators. The importance of the superintendent is obvious and well known.[15] He can initiate, advocate, mediate, or block activities in the school. The unflattering term "dinosaur" has come into common usage to describe the superintendent who views his main task as "keeping the lid on" and blocking efforts at change. Even when the superintendent serves as a change agent, there are other district administrators who can be "dinosaurs."

A recently completed case study of a large school district provides an example. Because of strong leadership from the superintendent, the district was highly successful in decentralizing much of its decision making to the school level, involving parents, teachers, the principal, and even students. Everything went well for at least two years, until those at the cabinet level—the various assistant superintendents—began to realize that their roles had changed significantly. They were responsible for serving the needs of others rather than directly making decisions for others to carry out. At this point these "leaders" became the major stumbling blocks to change.[16]

At the district level, there are additional influences brought to bear which affect the single school. Campbell and Layton catalog them as follows:

> Local political bodies and their leaders are drawn more and more into policy decisions, and religious bodies, patriotic societies, local universities, and civil rights groups are important in many communities. Citizens' school committees are often organized as watch-dog groups. The increasing cost of public education has brought greater activity by taxpayers' associations and other economic interest groups in some communities. Obviously, the voters in each school district, by holding ultimate control over local purse strings, have a kind of veto power over projected school policies.[17]

School districts have been fairly successful in controlling the involvement of boards, community groups, parents, and even teachers in the decision-making process, but this has been accomplished at the expense of openness. Rules, regulations, and policies have protected the system from interference. Withholding of information has been common. However, for a variety of reasons, such as community-involvement movements, teacher militancy, and scarce economic resources, these practices are breaking down.

There is much talk (and some action) about decentralizing educational decision making to the local school level. As a move toward building self-renewing skills, such decentralization is not only desirable, it is imperative. However, if district personnel on the one hand work for decentralization and on the other hand continue to operate a closed system, education may well be torn apart. Freedom and responsibility cannot be given in name only. We shall return to this issue in later chapters.

OTHER AGENCIES

There are countless agencies which are not arrayed in the hierarchy of educational decision making but which can and do affect what goes on in the school. Institutions of higher learning train teachers, administrators, and various educational specialists. In addition, they conduct research and produce knowledge directed at school improvement. Fortunately, spurred on by a lessened need for pre-service training, these institutions are turning more and more to the schools for guidance in designing their programs. It is no longer uncommon to see whole college and university training programs being conducted in the field. Likewise, it is not uncommon now to find university researchers looking at problems suggested by personnel in the schools. It is becoming less and less common to find researchers who enter a school, conduct a study, and return to the university to write up their results without any further contact with the school.

In addition to the colleges and universities there are many other agencies which provide services to schools on request. There are county offices, regional centers, regional laboratories, private consulting agencies, companies which produce materials and equipment, and professional associations with a variety of training programs. For the most part, such agencies produce knowledge or services. One of the major problems facing American education is how to have appropriate knowledge and services available to schools at the right time and in the right place. One generalization can be made at this point. If we are truly interested in developing self-renewing schools, there will have to be a closer link between knowledge-producing and service agencies and the schools.[18] Further, such a linkage will have to be interactive. In the past, producers of knowledge have tended to send that knowledge to users in the school with little or no attention to the process by which schools adopt and use the knowledge and with little or no concern for the real needs of the school. In the future, much more careful assessments of the need for knowledge and services of various kinds will have to be made. Such assessments, of necessity, will begin with the schools and will move outward to engage a variety of agencies in cooperative problem solving.

TOWARD A RATIONAL SET OF CHANGE STRATEGIES

We have tried to point out here that schooling involves decisions made at many levels of government. It is vastly more than a principal and a group of teachers in a single school, and it involves government at all levels. It involves literally millions of decisions made by the lay public, by administrators, and by intermediate educational agents who influence what the teacher can and does do. All these decisions restrict and compromise the workings of the individual school, and yet we feel that the single school is the unit that is critical in bringing about change and improving education. Strident cries for accountability and for decentralization are not enough to clarify the confusion in educational decision making. Telling the schools that they must implement national or state priorities cannot make them do so. The case of foreign language cited at the beginning of this chapter is a good example.

And yet, it is important that schools be responsive to national and state problems. We feel that two sets of conditions will have to be created before significant and lasting change will be brought about in schooling.

First, the schools themselves will need to become institutions concerned with purpose. This means that time must be provided and taken at the school level to discuss national and state priorities and that such discussions should result in action programs directed at meeting these priorities. For example, if conservation of resources is a priority, then programs in the school should reflect this need. Further, it means that all concerned actors will be involved in the process—teachers, administrators, students, parents, and community members. Also, it means that schools will link themselves to outside sources of knowledge and service as appropriate. Finally, it will mean that each school or network of schools will be encouraged, within broad policy and legal guidelines, to arrive at its own means of meeting such priorities.

There are limits to what the school can do in meeting national and state priorities. For example, the schools alone cannot overcome the evils of segregation. Neither can they alone break the cycle of poverty. Certainly, we agree that there should be equal educational opportunity for all, and we support the various plans which have been developed to provide the opportunity such as bussing and compensatory education. However, we would point out that societal problems cannot be left to the schools alone. Problems of equality of opportunity involve education, jobs, housing, medical care, the legal system, and a whole variety of other economic and social institutions. What the schools need are clear-cut policies which address themselves to our national and state priorities. To date, the various legislative, executive, and judicial actions regarding such matters as segregation have often been contradictory in nature. If the schools of the nation appear at times to be "drifting" or "mindless,"[19] it is at least in part because of the fact that superordinate institutions are also "drifting" and "mindless." The agencies which govern and serve the schools also must be concerned with purpose—their own, the nation's, and that of schools. Further, they need to have a much clearer understanding of just what role the schools can and should play in carrying out national purposes. For example, if a national purpose is to create better global understanding, then the place of foreign languages in the schools and the resources provided for its implementation should be reexamined thoughtfully with some notion as to what their introduction will do to the social system of the school.

We believe that to arrive at a meaningful set of change strategies for our schools, we must begin to think in terms of the separate but related roles of all of the actors in the educational drama. Thus, it is less a matter of discerning how to change schools and make them and the people in them more accountable than it is a matter of discerning what roles and accountabilities are appropriate for people at all levels of the system.

With this in mind, we propose that it should be the responsibility of sanctioning bodies—the public, their federal and state legislatures, and the courts—to clarify societal values through the passage of laws and to provide the necessary resources for their implementation. School boards should be responsible for a clear statement of enlightened educational aims derived from societal values and for guidelines for their implementation. The central staff of the school district should be responsible for stating institutional objectives derived from the statement of aims and for allocating human and financial resources and designing procedures for monitoring the accomplishment of objectives. Producers of knowledge—intermediate agencies such as universities and laboratories—should work closely with schools as they determine their needs, and such agencies should provide the schools with new skills and knowledge which will assist them in the solution of their real problems. For their part, teachers should be responsible for all instructional decisions, such as deriving instructional objectives from institutional objectives and bringing to bear appropriate learning resources and strategies. They should base these decisions upon an adequate knowledge of the content of instruction as well as an understanding of their students.

Within the framework proposed here, perhaps the responsibility of each agent can be limited to a clearly defined sphere.[20] Further, within such a framework, we perhaps can begin to design a set of change strategies that will allow us collectively to develop schools responsive to the needs of children and youth who are ultimately to be faced with their own changing world. It is within such a framework, then, that we can turn to the examination of existing change strategies in Chapter 6 and newer, emerging change strategies in Chapter 7. But before we do that, we must have some understanding of the change process itself and its meaning for schools. It is to this topic that we now turn.

NOTES

1   John B. Carroll, "Research on Teaching Foreign Languages," in Stanley Levenson and William Kendrick (eds.), *Readings in Foreign Languages for the Elementary School,* Blaisdell, Waltham, Mass., 1967. A recent study in Great Britain confirms these results. See Clare Burstall et al., *Primary French in the Balance,* NFER Publishing Co., Windsor, Berks, England, 1974.

2   Harold H. Howe, "Respect, Engagement, Responsibility," in *The Struggle for Power in the Public Schools,* National Committee for the Support of the Public Schools, Sixth Annual Conference Report, Washington, D.C., March 17–19, 1968, pp. 69–76.

3   For a contemporary and concise history of the U.S. Office of Education, including a discussion of the impact of ESEA, see Stephen K. Bailey, "The Office of Education and the Education Act of 1965," in Michael W. Kirst (ed.), *The Politics of Education at the Local, State and Federal Levels,* McCutchan Publishing Corporation, Berkeley, Calif., 1970.

4   *Rankings of the States, 1971* (also 1969 and 1970), National Education Association, Research Division, Washington, D.C., 1971.

5 See, for example, Sidney P. Marland, "A New Order for Educational Research and Development," *Phi Delta Kappan,* vol. 52, no. 10, pp. 576–579, June 1971.

6 Ann Hawley (ed.), *Contact Washington,* Washington Internship in Education, Washington, D.C., 1969.

7 Roald F. Campbell and Donald H. Layton, *Policy Making for American Education,* The University of Chicago, Midwest Administration Center, Chicago, 1969, p. 21.

8 See Albert H. Quie, "The Case for General Aid," and John Brademas, "The Case for Categorical Aid," in Kirst (ed.), op. cit.

9 Each year the Research Division, National Education Association, publishes a report, *High Spots in State Legislation.* This volume is recommended to those practitioners interested in how state legislatures affect education.

10 Campbell and Layton, op. cit., p. 20.

11 From an address on urban planning for education, delivered by Alex Mood, Bureau of Research, U.S. Office of Education, to Washington Interns in Education, Washington, D.C., January 1966.

12 Further information about the workings of the state level can be found in Roald F. Campbell and Tim L. Mazzoni, Jr. (eds.), *State Policy Making for the Public Schools: A Comparative Analysis,* Ohio State University, Educational Governance Project, Columbus, 1974.

13 See, for example, John I. Goodlad, M. Frances Klein, and Associates, *Looking Behind the Classroom Door,* rev. ed., Charles A. Jones Publishing Co., Worthington, Ohio, 1974. See also, Charles Silberman, *Crisis in the Classroom: The Remaking of American Education,* Random House, New York, 1970.

14 Kenneth A. Tye, "A Conceptual Framework for Political Analysis, Public Demands and School Board Decisions," unpublished doctoral dissertation, University of California, Los Angeles, 1968.

15 See, for example, Neal Gross, *Who Runs Our Schools?* Wiley, New York, 1958; Richard O. Carlson et al., *Change Processes in Public Schools,* Center for the Advanced Study of Educational Administration, Eugene, Oreg., 1965; and Richard O. Carlson, "School Superintendents and the Adoption of Modern Math: A Social Structures Profile," in Matthew B. Miles (ed.), *Innovation in Education,* Teachers College, New York, 1964.

16 Kenneth A. Tye, "The Process," unpublished case study, |I|D|E|A| Research Division, Los Angeles, 1972.

17 Campbell and Layton, op. cit., p. 18.

18 See Ronald G. Havelock, *Planning for Innovation through Dissemina-*

tion and Utilization of Knowledge, Center for Research on Utilization of Scientific Knowledge (CRUSK), Institute for Social Research, University of Michigan, Ann Arbor, 1971.

19 Silberman, op. cit.

20 See John I. Goodlad, "The Teacher Selects, Plans, Organizes," in *Learning and the Teacher,* Association for Supervision and Curriculum Development, Washington, D.C., 1959; and John I. Goodlad and Maurice N. Richter, Jr., *The Development of a Conceptual System for Dealing with Problems of Curriculum and Instruction,* U.S. Office of Education, Cooperative Research Report, SACE 8024, Project No. 454, 1967.

CHAPTER 5

THE SCHOOLS
AND CHANGE

Generally, it is not difficult to bring about indiscriminate change. One has merely to throw a lighted match into a warehouse of gunpowder and radical change will very likely result. Explosions, however, tend to cause havoc. The question is how change can be wrought in an orderly fashion to benefit the organization rather than destroy or harm it. As the authors of a 1969 book on planning change pointed out, "The predicament we confront . . . concerns method; methods that maximize freedom and limit as little as possible the potentialities of growth; methods that will realize man's dignity as well as bring into fruition desirable social goals."[1] A resolution of this predicament is still being sought, and hopefully will be found in the schools of the nation.

Unfortunately, change is frequently easier to sense than to define. Although we have long talked about and studied change, few succinct definitions have been attempted or perhaps even considered possible. For purposes of our discussion here, we will try to examine change as a concept in order to arrive at a common understanding of what it entails.

Change in its simplest form involves (a) energy input, (b) movement, and (c) time, and falls into the general category of "process." One might conceive of this process as analogous to a motion picture which in the long view catalogs a transition from one state of being to another but which in the shorter view is made up of a chronological sequence of moments, any one of which presents a slightly different picture than the one preceding it. Change always occurs within a context of vital environmental variables which interact, such as persons, things, and institutional processes, and it usually encounters resistance —anything in the environment which impedes the forward thrust of the change process (see Figure 5.1). By manipulating energy input, movement, time, or environmental factors, one can alter either the entire change process or elements of it.

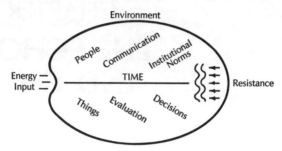

FIGURE 5.1 THE CHANGE PROCESS

This process often results in different degrees of impact. Chin defines five levels of change:[2]

1 Substitution: The simplest form of change in which one element is merely substituted for another that is already present (e.g., a new textbook is adopted, courses are rescheduled).

2 Alteration: Again, one element is substituted for another but, as a result, something is different (e.g., year-round school, alteration in graduation requirements).

3 Perturbations and Variations: Changes in performance which lead only to temporary shifts (e.g., double sessions, short-term experimental projects).

4 Restructuring: Changes which lead to a basic modification and reorganization of the structure (e.g., nongrading, team teaching, budget decentralization).

5 Value Reorientation: A reorganization and reappraisal of basic beliefs as to what comprises the good (e.g., a global curriculum orientation rather than a national one, personal development rather than intellectual development as an overarching goal of schooling, alternative programs rather than one "ideal" program).

Over the past five decades, various disciplines have been traveling similar paths toward what may eventually be a point of convergence on methods of managing change. The work in two such disciplines— business management and psychology—have particular relevance for schools.

In the early twentieth century, research and theory in business management, spurred on by rapidly advancing industrialization, led to the creation of the "scientific management" approach. Taylor, Fayol, and others carefully described what they saw as the essential mode of change in moving from an agricultural economy to one based upon industrial output.[3] Their prime concern was to discover ways of increasing production, but underlying this concern was the desire to promote and control large-scale change.

Although subsequent industrial movements were also concerned with increased production and the promotion of large-scale change, the "human relations" approach espoused by Mayo, Follett, and others in the late 1920s and early 1930s took a quite different position from the scientific management approach.[4] In discussing the human relations approach, Belisle and Sargent point out:

> We are really talking about . . . the continuously changing patterns of relationships among people. Structure and process have no other meaning and cannot really be differentiated; they are merely two sides of the same coin. And this coin is *language*, nothing else. All we can *observe* or *know* are dynamic patterns representing the configurations and flux of relationships among human beings. . . .
>
> If we think and devote our attention exclusively to development of relations with persons which permit them to be, spontaneously, *themselves*, mutually satisfying and productive relationships will thereby ensue between and among human beings. They will perpetuate the only "institution" worthy of survival—that of harmonious and creative relationships between self, others, and society.[5]

The more recent trends toward greater attention to the human side of enterprise as proposed by such people as McGregor and Argyris stress participative management as the means to increase both organizational production and change.[6] Interestingly, the scientific management and participative management movements are now confronting each other in American education. The movement toward accountability is based on scientific management principles. Participative management is represented in decentralization.

The field of psychology has also studied change, but here, of course, the focus is on the individual. Growing largely out of Freud's work and carried on in the work of Fromm, Jung, Sullivan, and Horney, psychology has concentrated on explaining the development of the human personality and its methods of coping with personal needs and anxiety.[7] The well-known Maslow hierarchy of needs is a conceptualization growing out of similar work.[8] The assumption underlying all these studies in the psychological realm was that once base-line data were determined, new methods and opportunities to help people change—or to help them cope with the change around them—would be available. The number of people currently seeing psychologists or psychiatrists on a regular clinical basis in part validates the assumption. The concern for adequate counseling services and the development of positive self-concepts of students is, likewise, evidence of the acceptance of such an assumption in schools.

THE EMERGING ANALYSIS OF CHANGE

As work in business management, psychology, and other fields such as anthropology, sociology, and political science has proceeded, it has gradually become clear that no single discipline or particular study has all the answers necessary to explain the phenomenon of change adequately. Nor does any single group have all the tools needed to control or manipulate its occurrence. The study of change has gradually emerged as a multidisciplinary endeavor in which the contributions of all have a place. A corollary development has been the emergence of bridging professions such as those of social psychologist, industrial psychologist, organizational development specialist, and public health expert, to mention only a few.

The work of one such individual, Kurt Lewin, a social psychologist interested in organizational development and change, has particular relevance. He defined organizational change as the altering of internal forces that support a particular kind of equilibrium so that one set of forces moves in to replace another.[9] In this definition, too, change involves energy input, movement of some kind, and some duration of time, whether the change involves persons, places, or things. Lewin's concept by implication also defines the status quo as a situation in which the forces promoting change are opposed by forces of equal strength which resist change. Lawrence Downey has diagramed these concepts as shown in Figure 5.2.

The notion is that if one is to cause change to occur, the ebb and flow of forces within the organization must be manipulated. As long as the forces of change and maintenance of the status quo are equal in strength, equilibrium, as represented by the center band, will be maintained. Purposeful alteration in either set of forces—through addition or subtraction—will cause the balance to be upset and change to occur.

A second major contribution to the study of change was made by

FACTORS ENCOURAGING CHANGE
Flexible role definition
Deviant group motives
Incompatible needs
Value conflict
Economic abundance

ORGANIZATION EQUILIBRIUM

E
N
D
S

Economic scarcity
Value similarity
Compatible needs
Conforming group motives
Inflexible role definitions
FACTORS PRESERVING THE STATUS QUO

FIGURE 5.2 ORGANIZATIONAL EQUILIBRIUM

From Lawrence W. Downey, "Organizational Theory as a Guide to Educational Change," *Educational Theory*, vol. 11, pp. 38–44, January 1961.

the team of Lippitt, Watson, and Wesley. Their book entitled *The Dynamics of Planned Change*,[10] published in the late 1950s, has become a classic in change literature. The book grew out of their study of the principles and techniques used in the work of various types of professional helpers concerned with change, and its conceptualization drew heavily upon Lewin's work. The authors identified and elaborated upon five general phases of the change process that must be recognized and understood by the change agent. We have adapted them as follows:

1 *Development of a need for change.* In any organization, including the school, an atmosphere must be created in which change is seen as possible and even desirable. Techniques for accomplishing this might include the use of brochures, memoranda, face-to-face discussions, demonstrations, consultation with groups who successfully instituted similar changes, or visits to other schools. Not all approaches will be successful with all groups, and methods must be chosen by a change agent in relation to the distinct qualities of the group. It is very important that the change agent be enthusiastic and dedicated to the proposed change. Also, personal reinforcement, by a principal of a school for example, can be the prime motivator in building staff dedication to the need for school change.

2 *The change relationship.* The change agent must clearly define his relationships to the change endeavor and to those involved in its accomplishment. Even in organizations where a preexisting relationship is broadly recognized—such as, for example, that which exists

between principal and teachers—any attempts to instigate and manage change must be accompanied by a clarification or redefinition of roles. Thus, the principal would want to make clear what he expects to do and what he expects of those with whom he is working.

Unfortunately, the desire for the benefits of a particular change is not always sufficient to move people into a "helping" frame of mind. Seasoned veterans of the organization, particularly if they have been through a series of change efforts, are usually not too anxious to jump on the bandwagon of another change promoter. This is especially true if they sense that the proposed changes are going to result in a new power balance. For the most part, the decision to be cooperative will correlate closely with whether or not individuals expect or hope to profit from the change. The wise change agent will carefully assess the motivational factors affecting his relationships with the staff. Valuable information can be gleaned simply by talking to personnel, looking carefully at change data, or examining individual commitments and responsibilities.

3 *Working toward change.* Once change has begun, it is critical that a staff remain vigorously and aggressively motivated. Large organizations in particular may be plagued with red tape which can easily stall or completely obliterate change efforts. Never should a change project be shunted aside or allowed to die on the vine. The inevitable outcome of beginning and not following through is the often-heard excuse, "We tried it, but it didn't work." There is no more effective mechanism for preventing or stalling future change. Sometimes, all that is required to keep motivation at a satisfactory level is reassurance and encouragement. At other times, a simple review of what has already been accomplished, in conjunction with a reevaluation of goals, will serve to keep things moving in the right direction. Above all, it is important at the outset of a change effort for people to recognize that they will stumble and that they may even fail, but that they can learn from their failures and what they learn will aid them in subsequent efforts.

4 *Generalization and stabilization of change.* Unless a change finds its way into the organizational bloodstream, it will not have a lasting impact. There is evidence to indicate that without integration of new structures into the existing system, organizations which seem to respond quite well to a change agent quickly return to their former way of operating as soon as the change agent leaves. Frequent and complete communication regarding goals and methods plus distribution of progress reports will aid immensely in preserving an implemented change. Of course, it is here that the practitioner as change agent can be much more effective than the outside "expert" who leaves after

the change has been implemented. However, care must be taken to help the organization maintain its independence so that the success of the change is not perceived as dependent upon the continuing presence or support of the change agent. A major part of any change agent's effort must be put into providing the organization with the means to solve its own problems as they come up.

5   *Achieving a terminal relationship.* Termination of an outside agent's services can occur at any one of the phases mentioned. The critical factor in termination is that self-sustaining mechanisms have been created. Sufficient independence and security must be fostered in the group so that it can take up new tasks and responsibilities without continued close supervision and support.

Any attempt to talk about the modern concern with change would be incomplete without mention of the book by Bennes, Benne, and Chin entitled *The Planning of Change.*[11] Originally published in 1961, the first edition had a heavy human-relations orientation, with much material derived from the work done at the National Training Laboratory. Included were such subjects as the roots of planned change, various models for change, and the interpersonal aspects of the change process. The second edition is a general source for the topic of planned change with particular emphasis on new and emerging practices of change planning. The differences between the two editions reflect, to a great extent, the enlarged view of change that developed in the 1960s.

The years between the editions witnessed increased concern among social scientists over the best means of moving organizations and individuals to adopt new and improved methods of operating. The role of the professional change agent has been more clearly delineated. The field of organizational development has brought into prominence the organizational development (OD) specialist whose prime responsibility it is to improve an organization's effectiveness and health. Beckhard, an OD theorist, points out that development of a strategy for systematic improvement of an organization demands that a change agent look carefully at the situation that currently exists, including an appraisal of the subsystems making up the overall institution and an examination of the processes occurring within the system, such as communication patterns and styles, relationships between groups, management of conflict, and the setting of goals.[12] Long-range beneficial change requires not only recognition of its necessity but a planned strategy for its achievement.

EDUCATIONAL CHANGE

What has been said above has for the most part had its genesis in fields apart from education. Oddly enough, educationists have only in recent years come to see the importance of integrating the knowledge of change and its processes into the school structure. Social and cultural pressures have forced us to confront our need to change.

Louis Rubin points out that schools move to institute change for three reasons: (1) what is proposed is clearly better than what it will replace, (2) what is proposed is sufficiently popular so that its absence is regarded as a sign of decadence, rigidity, or both, and (3) what is proposed will enhance the school's image as a modern, self-renewing institution.[13] Rubin breaks the change process into three steps: (1) preliminary analysis of the problem, (2) selection of an installing strategy which involves the determination of what change is to be made, who will direct it, and what circumstances surround the point of installation, and (3) action which puts the results of the previous steps into operation. Rubin is careful to point out that while these steps are not exclusive of each other and that considerable overlap will exist, chronological sequencing is important to prevent chaos. His primary plea is that the change process be approached with rationality and that any innovation be considered rationally in light of the needs and circumstances of each school.

Rationality, however, is not always easily applied to a changing school situation. Goodwin Watson comments that change is usually initiated because of outside rather than internal dissatisfaction.[14] School board members, superintendents, and parents, as well as teachers, custodians, and pupils all desire to see certain changes take place, but "they are not apt to express their desires for change."[15] What exists, then, is a potential readiness for change which can sometimes break through with surprising effects. The challenge for the change agent is to tap into this readiness and utilize it to propel movement toward change—without causing an explosion and uncontrollable upheaval.

In order to tap the latent desire of people for change and to involve them effectively in the processes of change, Rogers suggests that a way must be found to develop within the educational system as a whole, as well as in the various subunits, a climate which is not only conducive to personal growth but which actively fosters it. Rogers characterizes such a climate as one in which innovation is not frightening and in which the creative capacities of school personnel and students are nourished rather than stifled. As a means to achieving such a state, Rogers suggests the use of intensive group experience in what has been called encounter groups or T-groups. His point is that such training will help to develop individuals who are open to all of their experiences, aware of them and accepting, and who ultimately see themselves as continually in a process of change. These people can then bring about the creative educational organization that will also be continually in the process of changing.[16]

Jung goes a step further and advocates placing a person in the role of trainer within the school system whose function would be to concern himself with the phenomenon of change and with promoting awareness in persons throughout the system of their potential roles in relation to change. The assumption is that people need to be trained to use skills which make change possible.[17] Rogers and Jung reflect the National Training Laboratory (now the NTL Institute of Behavioral Sciences) approach to organizational change. The NTL intention was to use the dynamics of the group to train people to operate effectively in ambiguous and changing situations. The group was recognized as the link between the individual and the larger social structure. As a teaching device, group dynamics was intended to accomplish two broad goals: (1) the reeducation of an individual toward greater integrity, greater understanding of self and of the social conditions of his life, and greater behavioral effectiveness in planning and achieving changes both in himself and in his social environment; and (2) the formulation of changes in the larger social structure upon which individual lives depend.[18]

Sarason takes a different stance in regard to educational change: "One of the most difficult obstacles to recognizing that the major problems in our schools inhere far less in the characteristics of individuals than it does in its cultural and system characteristics is that one cannot see culture or system the way one sees individuals."[19] Sarason goes on to state that it is thus easier to think about an individual teacher or principal than it is to think about their roles within the system and their relationships independent of individual personalities. He observes that we do not have adequate knowledge of the actual functioning of schools and school systems and that change efforts in the educational context frequently come to naught because those attempting to bring change about do not understand the nature of the beast they are attempting to harness.

Miles, however, argues against assuming that the organizational properties of the school—such as decision-making methods and inter-personal climate—are simply there, that they are relatively invariant and cannot be made the subject of planned change efforts. He suggests that in order to predict the success of a change effort one must look at the organization's state of health, and that through improvement of organizational health one can make progress in attaining long-range change. He concludes that attention to organizational health ought to be of the highest priority for any administrator seriously concerned with innovation.[20]

Frymier, on the other hand, suggests that the school must be viewed as a social system, since it involves a number of people working together in cooperative ways to realize the attainment of some social end. He points out that viewing the educational enterprise through a social-system framework emphasizes that the power to improve and change inheres primarily in the *evaluation* phase of system operation. Evaluative feedback is the element which allows change to occur in a system, and it is precisely here that the educational system is deficient. There is no separate group in the educational hierarchy with the responsibility and the power of assessing the effectiveness of the total operation and that, consequently, is in a position to make the system improve and change through corrective feedback.[21]

A final note must be one of caution. Much has been written about educational change. A great deal more is presently in press. However, before taking it all to heart and barging headlong into the process, it is well to remember Downey's warning written early in the 1960s:

> Keen sensitivity as to the type and amount of disequilibrium appropriate to specific changes is the key to effective direction of change in an institution. Specifically, the innovator is advised to consider carefully the following minimal precautions:
>
> 1 Evaluate the worth of the basic idea itself, in terms of the school's purposes and in light of possible procedures for attaining it.
> 2 Evaluate the proposed innovation with the professional staff, not as an accomplished fact but rather in light of the need to be met and in terms of a possible procedure for meeting it.
> 3 Analyze the consequences for the formal organization. Define new roles and provide opportunities for training and experience in new relationships and new skills.
> 4 Anticipate the impact upon existing informal groups; assess the regrouping likely to be caused by the proposed change; and attempt to plan for the accommodation of emerging interactions.

5   Review individual needs and attempt to anticipate frustrations or threats created by the innovation; institute planned procedures for relieving anxieties.

6   Introduce the change on a trial basis. Failure in an experiment is not nearly as serious as failure in an adopted plan. Furthermore, a test run will provide opportunities for adjusting unanticipated consequences, for acquiring new skills, and for accommodating to new situations.[22]

Finally, Downey suggests that leadership is the most important prerequisite to successful change. The skillful leader estimates accurately his "degrees of freedom" for change and anticipates in detail the consequences for the organization and for individuals. He stands ready to fill any void which may be created by the change. He times his moves carefully. And when he moves he inspires in his followers the confidence necessary for success.

OBSTACLES TO CHANGE IN SCHOOLS

Understanding the concept of change and theories about how it occurs is not sufficient for the effective change agent. He must also understand that the school is full of obstacles which must be recognized and planned for if the change effort is to be successful. The obstacles most often encountered are those of (1) value dilemmas, (2) setting priorities, (3) vested interests, (4) the unresponsive bureaucracy, (5) the inappropriate solution, and (6) the leadership vacuum.

Value Dilemmas

Until recently, despite differences among Americans on many major issues, there has been widespread support of public education. Schooling was seen as the principal means of moving upward on social and economic ladders. It was also seen as the major vehicle for inculcating in our children and youth the values held in common by our society. However, in many areas it is no longer altogether clear what kind of society we want. We are caught on the horns of several dilemmas. Do we continue with increased technology and cybernation or do we move to a more person-centered society? Do we continue to believe in the "marketplace" or do we move to more highly centralized forms of long-range planning? Do we continue to believe in authority based upon voluntarily given respect? How can we seek unity within our society while also promoting diversity (pluralism)?[23] Such questions delve deeply into the operation of our schools. They question the value of work, our form of government, traditions, and heretofore commonly held beliefs. And our schools are trapped in a kind of inertia. They are constructed, organized, and staffed so that their programs will inculcate those values which have gone before. If they do not reject, they certainly do not promote emerging values.

Even so, we can more than likely find widespread agreement among most Americans regarding the lofty, long-standing aims of American schooling. A common set of goals would include such things as (1) learning the basic skills of reading, writing, speaking, listening, and computing; (2) learning to understand and practice the principles of good citizenship; (3) developing sound mental and physical health; (4) learning how to earn a living in work for which one is suited; (5) developing oneself as a worthwhile, contributing person; (6) developing desirable habits, attitudes, and understandings related to the use of leisure time; (7) perceiving and enjoying beauty in everyday life; (8) thinking critically as a basis of intelligent action; (9) understanding other peoples of the world.

Almost every school or school district has a document which contains statements of aims, goals, or beliefs such as those above. However, when we look at those statements in light of what they really mean for school practice, we are not always so sure of what we want. Let us take just two examples to demonstrate the dilemma: integration and sex education.

In 1954 the U.S. Supreme Court charged the nation with the responsibility of desegregating its schools. The Civil Rights Act of 1964 reinforced and put more teeth into this responsibility. During the past decade, court case after court case has pushed forward this apparent societal mandate for schooling. And yet, in recent national and local elections we have found politicians campaigning against bussing designed to accomplish desegregation because those politicians placed the value of freedom of choice above that of equality of opportunity. Because of this conflict of values and because the value of freedom of choice is more "traditional" than that of equality of opportunity, one has to look far and wide to find school districts which will voluntarily integrate their schools without actually being under court order to do so.

Sex education offers another example. It is probably safe to say that sex education in the schools is widely supported by the American people. However, it is probably also true that the majority of Americans do not wish their children to be taught about sex without that teaching being cast in some value framework. And yet, without universal agreement about such matters as abstinence, birth control, or abortion, what values do we expect the schools to promote?

Integration and sex education are only two of the many dilemmas faced by school people. Others include the value of work versus the value of leisure time, nationalism versus internationalism, economic development versus conservation, freedom of protest versus law and order, traditional family roles versus women's rights, self-reliance versus cooperation, and self-direction versus reliance upon authority. Frequently, educators attempt to deal with these dilemmas by "teaching about" value differences or by using their own values, believing them to be bias-free and acceptable. Too often, such an approach results in nothing more than an obscure, confused, or unreal picture of our society and the world.

Such value dilemmas will be faced by schools for years to come, and those in the schools will have to deal with them. They have several choices. They can be advocates of certain values. They can design alternative programs based upon divergent values from which parents and students can choose. They can involve their local communities in discussions of critical values from which programs can be designed. Or they can do nothing themselves and react to pressures as they arise. However, whatever is done should be done consciously with some perspective of the future, some view of the societal role of schooling, and some understanding of the value dilemmas faced by society.

Establishing Priorities

The matter of financing education has brought into sharp focus our basic commitment as a people to universal public education. Immediately after World War II, there was a great faith in education as a means to better the individual and the nation. Public Laws 874 and 815 supported expanded programs and school construction. The National Defense Education Act (NDEA) provided financial support for existing programs. Local and state contributions to education rose dramatically.

By 1965, with the passage of the Elementary and Secondary Education Act (ESEA) and the Higher Education Act (HEA), the people of the United States had made a historic commitment to education. This was done while simultaneously overcoming the historical roadblocks standing in the way of federal aid—local control, separation of church and state, and civil rights. But this scene has changed.

At the time of the passage of ESEA, HEA, and other federal legislation, the economy of the United States appeared to be quite healthy and it was expected to continue to grow. Therefore, it was generally assumed that federal financial support of educational programs would increase significantly as the years passed. For example, Title III of ESEA, which was designed specifically to encourage educational innovation, received $75 million during fiscal year 1966. This was raised to $145 million during fiscal year 1967. Those who administered the program at that time planned on the basis of the following suggested budgets for the next five years:[24]

Fiscal Year	Millions
1968	$ 250
1969	630
1970	1,500
1971	2,000
1972	2,200

Based upon such projections, numerous projects were approved and funds committed during fiscal 1966 and 1967 for periods of up to three years. Many of these early projects were far from innovative and some were funded primarily on the basis of state dollar quotas. But they were a beginning. The notion was that new and better projects would be funded in subsequent years from increased funds made available by Congress, while, at the same time, original projects would be completed.

By fiscal 1972, however, funding for Title III-ESEA was actually only $146.25 million, or only slightly more than one million dollars above the 1967 funding level. This was a far cry from the $2.2 billion projected for fiscal 1972 some five years earlier.

The war in Indochina, inflation at home, the generally depressed economy, and intense competition among social services for scarce tax dollars—all have caused federal spending for education to remain constant or to rise only slightly over the past several years.

The educational finance picture is even gloomier when state and local levels are considered. Without the anticipated massive infusion of federal monies into education, state and local governments have had to rely upon traditional and already burdened sources of income in order to finance public education—sales taxes and property taxes.

Again, with inflation and intensified competition for funding for social services at these governmental levels, education has not fared well. In Los Angeles in 1971, for example, the city raised property taxes some 3 percent. The county followed suit by approving a rate increase of 9 percent. Neither raise in rate required the vote of the people. When the independent Los Angeles City Schools proposed a tax increase, the voters turned it down overwhelmingly, for the eighth straight year! And the picture is much the same all across the nation, with many school districts on the verge of bankruptcy, cutting deeply into existing programs in order to keep schools open on some minimum basis. As Chapter 3 pointed out, this poses great problems for schools in dealing with their communities.

Since a depressed economy and restricted funding are facts of life in the United States right now, priorities will have to be set for the use of funds that are available. Do we value education per se, and if so, are we willing to support it financially? Or, perhaps, education is somewhat less important than defense, health, environment, crime prevention, housing, transportation, or even access to alcohol and tobacco. Whatever the case, priorities must be set so that limited financial resources can be allocated reasonably within some sense of national and state importance so that those who operate institutions will know what resources are available as they, in turn, work toward the establishment of priorities.

Given some sense of resource availability, those who make decisions about the effectiveness of schooling can begin to make decisions about resource investment. How much and what kind of research is needed? Should schooling be extended downward, upward? What kinds of equipment, materials, and facilities are desirable? How can staff be trained and for what? What kind of staff should be employed? How desirable, in reality, is foreign language instruction for all children? If we could set priorities and then consider available resources, we might avoid the somewhat ludicrous practice of cutting all existing programs by 5, 10, or 20 percent when resources become short. However, herein resides another barrier to change, vested interests.

Vested Interests

When the role of the school is seen as anything more than transmitting the culture, the problem of vested interests arises immediately. For if there is to be an alteration in any phase of life—job opportunity, economic wealth, social status, for example—for one group of people, it is easy for another group of people to perceive that they stand to lose something. One or another group will always have personal commitments—economic, cultural, ethnic, psychological—either to things as they are (the status quo), or to things as they might be if the change they want were initiated. The endorsement of educational innovation "as long as it doesn't raise taxes" is an obvious and widespread form of vested interest which inhibits reform. Some segments of society view higher taxes for education as a means of taking material benefits away from them. In those states (e.g., California, Minnesota, New Jersey, and Texas) where there is discussion of statewide equalization of the distribution of property taxes for education, many people in "richer" districts are openly and loudly fighting such equalization on the grounds that their own taxes will rise. The question is openly asked, "Why should I pay for the education of other people's children?"

The fear of white parents, real or rationalized, that school integration will lower the quality of education for their children is another example of vested interest. While most people can and do agree in principle with the desirability of integration, when it comes to such things as the resale value of their own houses or the education of their own children, they are frequently far from willing to make any personal sacrifices for the common good.

There are countless other examples of vested interests in society which frequently stand in the way of or, in many cases, promote specific educational changes. Lobbies and special interest groups at the national and state levels and organized groups at the local level exert significant pressures in their own areas of interest. These include suppliers of services and goods to schools, insurance companies which want driver education or private driver training companies which do not want driver education, parents or others who have specific religious beliefs, unions which do or do not wish certain kinds of vocational training programs, specialized schooling groups (e.g., business educators, physical education teachers, counselors), and the like.

Often, school people react prematurely to vested interests they perceive to exist in society. An example can be found in the matter of planning time for teachers. Almost all educators agree that there should be some type of periodic early dismissal for students so that teachers can have adequate time for planning. The major stumbling block to such a change is not money; rather, it is the assumption on the part of administrators that parents will object to periodic early dismissal of students because such dismissal will interfere with the work or social activities of parents. Although this is a real problem, many schools, in fact, have altered schedules to allow for teacher planning time. The year-round school, now in operation in many school districts of the nation, is an even more radical schedule change which indicates that some perceived or real vested interests can be overcome if necessary as long as there is adequate planning and communication between school people and the public.

Our traditions at times take on the mantle of vested interest. Michael has pointed out that men in organizations spend years learning successful behavior and developing self-satisfying images. The tendency then is to protect this success by making present institutional formats work with minimum change.[25] Overcoming the human tendency to guard one's own interests takes much time and a good deal of reeducation of all involved. The case of the assistant superintendents described in Chapter 4 is an example. When they found that their roles had changed from leadership to serving the needs of others because of the district's decentralization plan, they began to block the change that they themselves had helped initiate.

The Unresponsive Bureaucracy

In the study of demands made upon the Los Angeles City Schools, cited earlier, it was found that of the nearly 2,000 demands presented to the Board of Education in one year, only 7.3 percent were immediately acted upon. Others were referred to committee or to the superintendent (31.8 percent). Another 44.7 percent were simply acknowledged by the board president or board clerk. The remaining demands were not acted upon at all (16.2 percent), although they were more than likely "taken under advisement."[26]

Statistics aside, there is a prevailing general feeling that large school systems are very unresponsive to the public and its wishes. And there is much evidence to support such feelings.

To date, the most rational method known to man for ensuring the accomplishment of his institutional purposes is to establish bureaucratic structures. Such structures are effective in maintaining order and control and in implementing common means to accomplish common purposes. Because of this, schools have become highly bureaucratized units within highly bureaucratized school districts. Standards of attainment are common for all or most pupils. What is to be taught and how it is to be taught are dictated by state or district syllabi or state-adopted commercial textbooks. Policy, rules, and regulations abound and tend to be restrictive and to mitigate against any form of change. Line and staff arrangements are frequently so complex that it is difficult to find anyone who has the actual authority or responsibility for taking action on any given matter. The "gatekeepers" of the system, those who defend it from outside intrusion, are often very effective. Parents and other community members are often frustrated again and again when they attempt to get information or when they seek some type of action.

Beyond formal rules and regulations, there are subtle and powerful informal means by which bureaucratic organizations inhibit innovation. Norms, which are customary and expected ways of behaving, grow up over the years. Watson lists time schedules; modes of dress; forms of address to colleagues, superiors, and subordinates; indications of institutional loyalty; personal ambition to rise; appropriate consumption; and forms of approved participation in recreation and community life as powerful norms which inhibit change in bureaucratic institutions.[27]

Because the majority of individuals within an organization share norms, those who advocate change or who deviate from these norms will either be pressured to conform or will be ignored or excluded. Even institutions which have been set apart with sanctions to operate differently for a time tend ultimately to be forced to conform to the norms of the greater system.[28]

Nothing short of altering the bureaucratic structures of educational institutions will suffice if we are really committed to significant educational improvement. As suggested in Chapter 4, we need structures which will allow for participatory decision making at levels other than at the top. Such decision making would include not only teachers and students at the local school but parents and community members as well. There is much movement now in this direction; some of it is troublesome, but much of it is promising.

The Inappropriate Solution

Another reactive move which schools are frequently guilty of is making changes in response to some perceived problem without clearly thinking through the purposes or needs of the students and local community. In many instances, such changes are made arbitrarily without adequate involvement of the community. For example, in response to the problem of low standardized-test scores, new reading or math programs might be adopted, television employed, modular scheduling utilized, or foreign language requirements altered, none of which actions might have any success in solving the problem. They do, however, have the virtue of making the school appear to be doing something. In defense of school people, it must be stated that such changes are usually perceived as ways of improving the educational program or as ways of overcoming some deficiency which has existed. The fact that such changes don't often seem to bring about the needed improvement and that the community sometimes reacts negatively is often perplexing to school people.

School people are decision oriented. In fact, most of their working time is spent in making decisions. Thus, it is natural for them to react to some perceived need by deciding to use an alternative solution. By and large, school people are neither trained nor encouraged to utilize more complex diagnostic or problem-solving behavior, the kind of behavior needed in a complex society.

Problem-solving behavior can be an orderly step-by-step procedure or it can be less formal. The advocates of action research suggest the following simple steps when a problem arises:[29]

> Selection of a specific problem and the formulation of a hypothesis which implies a goal and a procedure for reaching it.
> Careful recording of actions (procedure) and accumulation of evidence to determine the degree to which the goal is reached.
> Inferring generalizations from the evidence about the relation between the action and the desired goal.
> Continually retesting the generalizations in other action situations.

For example, a school might not be satisfied with the results of its present reading program. Analysis of test results and discussion reveal that by the end of four years approximately half of its students do not have adequate reading skills or the ability to apply reading skills to problem-solving activities. There are three obvious alternatives. First, the school can intensify its present efforts. Second, it can discard its present program and arbitrarily adopt a new program, risking the inappropriate solution. Third, it can create a program of action research.

If the school selects the third alternative it initiates the steps suggested above. Once the problem has been identified, a hypothesis is stated. For example, it might be hypothesized that if we use a language-experience approach to reading, then at the end of four years we will expect students to develop more concepts through reading. To bring this change about we will select more and better books to read and we shall anticipate that 95 percent of all students will comprehend reading material at or above age-level expectancy when their ability is measured by standardized reading tests.

Once procedures for the program are established and teachers are trained in their use, a group of children is selected for the program. Records are kept on classroom procedures, concept development of students is measured over the four-year period, records are kept of books read by children, and standardized tests are administered.

At the end of four years, evidence about the program is gathered and tentative generalizations are stated. For example, it might be observed that when the language-experience approach is used with a certain type of student, concept development is greater and book selection is better, but comprehension as measured by standardized tests is not markedly increased. Further analysis might show, however, that little attention was given to the procedure of contextual analysis, which would bear directly on comprehension, at later stages in the program. A linguistic program and phonics program or combination of various programs can be researched at the same time. Ultimately, a problem-solving approach to instruction can reap great rewards in the form of improved programs.[30] And if the community is kept informed and involved appropriately at each step along the way, the odds are that they will be both understanding and supportive of the changes brought about.

The Leadership Vacuum

Lipham, in writing about educational leadership, distinguishes between the roles of administrators and leaders.[31] He points out that a leader is primarily concerned with the creation of new structures or procedures for achieving the goals of the institution or with the establishment of new goals for that institution. The role of the administrator is to use existing structures and procedures to achieve existing goals. The fact is that most people in key roles in education have been educated and have gained reinforcing experiences as administrators and therefore lack leadership skills and motivations.

By and large, school administrators are selected from the ranks of those who have been successful teachers. This, in itself, is a problem, as Michael observes:

> Most of today's teachers and educational administrators were themselves educated, and are still being educated, on the basis of social perspectives that are insensitive to the cognitive and emotional requirements for a [changing society]. Most primary and secondary school teachers . . . come from backgrounds more at ease with a conservative view of life, suspicious of the strange, the innovative, the spontaneous, comfortable with the requirements, certainties, rewards, and the moral assurance of the Protestant ethic. Hence, there is no reason to suppose that, short of disaster, major, widespread changes are likely to be the lot of education in general over the next decade at least.[32]

School administrators, after being successful teachers, are trained in such subjects as educational law, school governance, supervision, educational business procedures, and school curriculum. Generally, this training consists of "how to do it," and these "how to do its" are derived from past and present practice. Seldom is any of this training couched in systems-thinking, which deals with the relationships among variables, cause and effect, or prediction. Change as a social or educational phenomenon is hardly ever included in any training for those who do or will hold key positions in education. The result is that school administrators use the past as a data source as they attempt to deal with the present and to plan—if they do—for the future. They rely on policy and regulations to conserve the values, attitudes, and procedures which have made schools successful in the past. However, as conditions change, what was successful in the past may well not be successful tomorrow. We need to develop a cadre of educational leaders who know how to plan, who know how to work with and influence others, who keep abreast of new educational developments, and who see schooling as one functioning part of a broader social, political, and economic context. Then, perhaps education will move forward.

We assume that if you are reading this book, you have made a commitment to bringing about change and promoting innovation in education. We have discussed here the concept of change itself and some of the obstacles to change which may be encountered. We turn now to a consideration of the strategies that are available for instituting change—both those now in use and those of the future which offer promise for solving our education dilemmas.

NOTES

1   Warren G. Bennes, Kenneth D. Benne, and Robert Chin, *The Planning of Change*, 2d ed., Holt, New York, 1969, p. 2.

2   Robert Chin, "Models and Ideas about Changing," in W. C. Meierhenry (ed.), *Media and Educational Innovation*, University of Nebraska Press, Lincoln, 1963.

3   See, for example, Frederick W. Taylor, *Scientific Management*, Harper & Row, New York, 1947; and Henri Fayol, *General and Industrial Management*, Pitman & Sons, London, 1949.

4   See, for example, Elton Mayo, *The Human Problems of an Industrial Civilization*, Harvard University, Boston Graduate School of Business Administration, Cambridge, Mass., 1946; and Mary Parker Follett, *Creative Experience*, Longmans, London, 1924.

5   Eugene L. Belisle and Cyril G. Sargent, "The Concept of Administration," in Roald F. Campbell and Russell T. Gregg (eds.), *Administrative Behavior in Education*, Harper & Row, New York, 1957, pp. 110–111.

6   See, for example, Douglas McGregor, *The Human Side of Enterprise*, McGraw-Hill, New York, 1960; and Chris Argyris, *Personality and Organization: The Conflict between System and the Individual*, Harper & Row, New York, 1957.

7   For additional information, see Calvin S. Hall and Gardner Lindzey, *Theories of Personality*, Wiley, New York, 1957.

8   Abraham Maslow, "A Theory of Human Motivation," *Psychological Review*, vol. 50, pp. 370–396, 1943.

9   Information on Lewin's work may be found in Alfred Marrow, *The Practical Theorist: The Life and Work of Kurt Lewin*, Basic Books, New York, 1969. For a discussion of disequilibrium and its management in the change process, see Kenneth A. Tye, "Creating Disequilibrium," in Jerrold M. Novotney (ed.), *The Principal and the Challenge of Change*, monograph, |I|D|E|A|, Melbourne, Fla., 1968.

10   Ronald Lippitt, Jeanne Watson, and Bruce Wesley, *The Dynamics of Planned Change*, Harcourt, Brace & World, New York, 1958.

11   Bennes, Benne, and Chin, op. cit.

12   Richard Beckhard, *Organizational Development, Strategies and Methods*, Addison-Wesley, Reading, Mass., 1969.

13   See, Louis J. Rubin, *Facts and Feelings in the Classroom*, Walker, New York, 1973.

14   Goodwin Watson, "Toward a Conceptual Architecture of a Self-Renewing School System," in Goodwin Watson (ed.), *Change in*

School Systems, National Training Laboratory, Washington, D.C., 1967.

15 Ibid., p. 107.

16 Carl R. Rogers, "A Practical Plan for Educational Revolution," in Richard R. Goulet (ed.), *Educational Change: The Reality and the Promise,* Citation Press, New York, 1968.

17 Charles C. Jung, "The Trainer Change Agent Role within a School System," in Watson (ed.), op. cit.

18 See, Leland P. Bradford, Jock R. Gibb, and Kenneth D. Benne, *T-Group Theory and Laboratory Method,* Wiley, New York, 1964; and Jerrold M. Novotney, "T-Groups and Team Teaching," *The California Journal for Instructional Improvement,* vol. 10, pp. 242–247, December 1967.

19 Seymour B. Sarason, *The Culture of the School and the Problem of Change,* Allyn and Bacon, Boston, 1971, p. 228.

20 Matthew B. Miles, "Planned Change and Organizational Health: Figure and Ground," in Richard O. Carlson (ed.), *Change Processes in the Public Schools,* Center for the Advanced Study of Educational Administration, University of Oregon Press, Eugene, 1969.

21 Jack R. Frymier, *Fostering Educational Change,* Charles E. Merrill Books, Inc., Columbus, Ohio, 1969.

22 Lawrence W. Downey, "Direction Amid Change," *Phi Delta Kappan,* February 1961, p. 189.

23 For an extensive review of these and other value dilemmas facing American education, see Willis W. Harman, *The Nature of Our Changing Society: Implications for Schools,* ERIC Clearinghouse on Educational Administration, Eugene, Oregon, 1969.

24 Commitee on Labor and Public Welfare, United States Senate, *Catalyst for Change: A National Study of ESEA Title III,* 1967, p. 93.

25 Donald R. Michael, "Factors Inhibiting and Facilitating the Acceptance of Educational Innovations," University of California, Institute of Government and Public Affairs, Los Angeles, 1964.

26 Kenneth A. Tye, "A Conceptual Framework for Political Analysis, Public Demands and School Board Decisions," unpublished doctoral dissertation, University of California, Los Angeles, 1968.

27 Goodwin Watson, "Resistance to Change," in Goodwin Watson (ed.), *Concepts for Social Change,* National Education Association, National Training Laboratory, Institute for Applied Behavioral Science, Washington, D.C., 1967.

28 For example, see the literature on what happened to experimental

schools and colleges in Matthew B. Miles (ed.), *Innovation in Education,* Teachers College, New York, 1964.

29   Arno Bellack et al., "Action Research in Schools," *Teachers College Record,* vol. 54, pp. 246–255, 1953. See also, Stephen M. Corey, *Action Research to Improve School Practices,* Teachers College, New York, 1953.

30   The example used here is taken from Tye, "Creating Disequilibrium," op. cit.

31   James M. Lipham, "Leadership and Administration," in *Behavioral Science and Educational Administration,* National Society for the Study of Education, Sixty-third Yearbook, Part II, The University of Chicago Press, Chicago, 1964.

32   Donald R. Michael, *The Unprepared Society: Planning for a Precarious Future,* Basic Books, New York, 1968, p. 114.

CHAPTER 6
OUR PRESENT CHANGE STRATEGIES

In the fall of 1967, when Title III of the Elementary and Secondary Education Act was entering its third year of operation, the administrators of the program finally commissioned a position paper on the process of educational change that was to include specific recommendations on the implementation of Title III.[1] Thus, for two years, monies had been allocated to encourage educational change with very little thought given to how such change takes place and without much reference to existing knowledge about change.

Morris Janowitz observed that prior to 1969 most efforts to change schools were piecemeal and were frequently directed toward the development of model demonstration projects of one kind or other rather than toward planning fundamental institution building. As a result, these projects had little overall impact:

> They have tended generally to be small scale and short lived, with professionals learning that results are not cumulative but rather seem to be disjunctive. There is a high turnover of personnel so that the consequences of a particular demonstration face gradual extinction. . . . After a decision to spread the demonstration project throughout the system, it faces death by diffuse and partial incorporation.[2]

For nearly a decade, our efforts in educational change have put the cart before the horse. Because the national interest and investment in educational change came on so quickly in the mid-sixties, educators at all levels were ill-prepared to take advantage of that interest and investment. Educational change projects were instituted willy-nilly with little planning and, therefore, little result.

Since 1969, a few well-defined change models have been utilized in various schools and school districts around the country. In the remainder of this chapter, we will examine a number of these. The models which will be discussed are: (1) the use of authority and influence, (2) the marketing strategy, (3) the research, development, and diffusion strategy, (4) the change-agent strategy, and (5) the problem-solving strategy. These strategies are distinguished from those to be dealt with in Chapter 7 because they have all been tested and have been found to be at least partially effective in bringing about change in schools.

THE USE OF AUTHORITY AND INFLUENCE

The most common means used to bring about change in the schools is for someone in a position of recognized authority to tell someone else with less authority to behave in a new or different manner (see Figure 6.1). Thus, it is not uncommon to see a new syllabus or course of study prepared at the district level and disseminated to all teachers to be implemented in their classrooms. Neither is it uncommon for a state legislature, city council, school board, superintendent of schools, or school principal to formulate a new policy or regulation which must be adhered to by teachers. Finally, in cases where community groups are perceived as having or actually do have authority, they, too, may "pass down" new ideas for teachers to implement. Similarly, authority can be used to maintain the status quo.

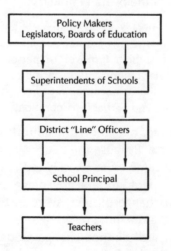

FIGURE 6.1   THE TRADITIONAL FLOW OF AUTHORITY IN SCHOOLING

In our schools, as in most institutions, there are some people or bodies who are perceived as having power or authority over others in the form of rewards, promotions, change of assignments, dismissals, good evaluations, or bad evaluations. Thus, the principal or teacher who does not comply with policies or regulations set down by superordinates risks the loss of many advantages which he or she might obtain otherwise.

The use of authority is hardly ever as straightforward as has been briefly described here. More often than not it is subtle or even devious. Behind a screen of ostensibly democratic practices, paternalism or manipulation are often at work. Under a paternalistic system, the person in authority allows others to do what they wish as long as it agrees with his own values, policies, or regulations. Also, the person in authority rewards his subordinates for what he considers their "right" actions. There are many reasons why people in authority positions behave in a paternalistic manner. Ego needs are involved, as are fears of losing control of the situation. Lack of faith or trust in others is also a reason. Most insidious, of course, is the fact that in many systems paternalism is encouraged or rewarded. Thus, the principal who deals with his teachers in a paternalistic manner may be doing so because the board and the superintendent have established such behavior as the only acceptable mode for those in positions of authority.

To some degree all of us attempt to manipulate other human beings. In the best sense, for example, parents attempt to manipulate their children so that they can have positive, growthful experiences. The same is true of the teacher. Those who object to the term or the actual act of manipulation do so usually because it implies one person having some form of control over another. Further, they suggest that manipulation more often than not implies some form of deceit.

Regardless of whether we view manipulation as good or bad, the fact is that those in authority in education frequently do manipulate others in an attempt to control their behavior. Principals, for example, frequently have control over the allocation of resources to teachers. Also, they frequently assign rooms to teachers and students to classes. They arrange visits for teachers. They make countless other decisions which can be viewed as giving rewards. If a principal gives such rewards only to those who agree with his views or to those who are friendly, supportive, or who otherwise behave in concert with norms he sees as desirable, then it can be said that he is attempting to manipulate or coerce others into behaving in certain ways.

There are various forms of influence which people in positions of authority can and do use legitimately to create change in a system.[3] For example, when someone who is perceived as possessing superior knowledge or ability is called upon to speak, advise, or consult on a given subject, he is using *expert influence*. Despite the fact that behavioral scientists consider this form of influence to be weak compared to others, educators rely heavily upon so-called experts. Calling in a consultant has become commonplace in American education.

Legitimate influence is very important to those in positions of authority. It implies that subordinates view those above them in the line organization as having the right to prescribe attitudes and behaviors for them. The critical element in such a perception is that subordinates view their superordinates as having "earned" the right to use the influence of their positions. Without this element, those in authority are not perceived as legitimate, regardless of their title. Thus, in education it often becomes very important for principals and other authority figures to be able to demonstrate that they were "good" teachers and, in fact, that they worked up through the ranks. In many respects, there is validity to this kind of argument. Too frequently, those who have not been practitioners (e.g., university theoreticians or laymen) develop simplistic panaceas for educational problems which tend to overlook factors which are obvious to practitioners. The advocacy of phonics as a cure-all for all reading deficiencies is an example. Beginning reading is a far more complicated matter than adopting one particular methodology, and those who have practiced know this.

On the other hand, total reliance upon legitimate influence is not good either because it tends to close the system and does not allow for new ideas to be brought in from the outside.

Another powerful type of influence which operates in our school systems is *referent influence*. People have a natural tendency to want to test their own attitudes, beliefs, and behaviors on those with whom they identify closely. Therefore, teachers will be more open to discussing new ideas with other teachers, and principals to dealing with other principals. One of the most promising developments of the past decade is the emergence of Teachers' Centres in Great Britain.[4] Run primarily by the Teachers' Union, but with support from local education authorities, these centers find teachers sharing ideas, establishing their own workshops, and working together in many ways. Another similar movement is that of the Association of California School Administrators (ACSA) through its Project Leadership.[5] In this project, the professional administrators' association, with support from various districts, is assisting its members to upgrade their own skills.

The use of authority as a change strategy, utilizing paternalism, manipulation, influence, or even outright tyranny, has some advantages. Since there is only one source of decisions, there is usually clarity of expectations. With such clarity, it is also probable that actions can be carried out expeditiously and without question. However, there are a number of significant problems connected with the use of authority as the basis for making changes in schooling. People who work in a situation where decisions are made for them can become dependent and even lethargic. The human desire to be creative can be lessened, at least in the work situation. People can become closed or resistant to change or direction, or they can organize their own power group to counter the authority of those who are in positions of power.

The manner in which we view other people perhaps best dictates how we view the use of authority as a means for bringing about change in schools. McGregor points out that organizations develop a kind of "self-fulfilling prophecy." In an organization where people are not trusted and are viewed as inferior, lazy, materialistic, dependent, and resistant to change, they become so. When they are trusted and viewed as responsible, independent, understanding, goal-achieving, growing, and creative, they will display these attributes.[6] McGregor calls the first kind of organization "X-minded." The organization in which there is trust he refers to as "Y-minded." We have adapted his description of these organizations to schools:

Behaviors Manifested in a School Staffed by X-minded People	**Behaviors Manifested in a School Staffed by Y-minded People**
The promotion of the dependency of children upon adults for direction, and the dependency of teachers upon administrators for direction.	The promotion of the independence, self-fulfillment, and responsibility of children by teachers and of teachers by administrators.
The utilization of extrinsic rewards and punishments such as grades and promotion or firing for teachers.	The reliance upon intrinsic reward systems for children and teachers, such as pride in achievement, enjoyment of process, sense of contribution, pleasure of association, and stimulation of new challenges.
The emphasis upon telling, show-	An emphasis upon children and

ing, and training in how to do it and in proper methods of work for both children and teachers.

teachers devising their own methods of work and gaining ever-increasing understanding of the activities in which they engage.

The reliance upon teachers who watch children closely enough to praise good work and reprimand errors, and upon supervisors who do the same to teachers.

The building of an atmosphere in which children and teachers sense that they are respected as capable of assuming responsibility for self-correction.

The advancement of the belief that work, with learning as a form of work, is somehow separated from the leisure activities of both children and teachers.

The advancement of the belief that work, with learning as a form of work, is a lifelong pursuit and is inextricably interwoven with the leisure activities c both children and teachers.

The fostering of the idea that jobs and learnings are primary and must be done, and that people (teachers and children) are selected, trained, and fitted to predefined jobs and learnings.

The fostering of the idea that teachers and children are primary and seek self-realization, and that jobs and learning must be designed, modified, and fitted to people.

The feeling that children and teachers need to be inspired or pushed or driven to accomplish goals external to themselves and their settings.

The feeling that children and teachers need to be released and encouraged and assisted as they set about accomplishing their own goals.

The assumption that children and teachers prefer familiar routines; they thrive on the "tried and true."

The assumption that children and teachers naturally tire of monotonous routine and enjoy new experiences; to some degree everyone is creative.[7]

School districts and schools are fraught with traditions and bureaucratic structures which tend to make them authoritarian. In such situations, some change is possible, to be sure. However, as we face the tremendous social and technological changes of the future, it is doubtful that authoritarian models will create any significant and responsive improvements in the schools of America. Because of his mode of operation, the authoritarian has to preoccupy himself with keeping his position and power, which can only lead to the maintenance of the status quo. Also, because it sets the tone for what happens to children in the classroom, perhaps the most significant change which could occur in our schools is the elimination of just these authoritarian practices. A beginning point for those who now possess authority is for them to recognize and behave as if they were in a "Y-minded" organization.

THE MARKETING STRATEGY

In our materially oriented society, we have a preoccupation with the "things" of schooling. There are more instructional materials and equipment in our classrooms than in any other classrooms in the world. One major strategy for changing our schools, therefore, has been the improvement of the instructional materials and equipment used in the classroom. By and large, such materials and equipment have been developed outside of the system, mainly by commercial interests, though the strategy has had the direct support of the federal government through the National Defense Education Act (NDEA), Title II of the Elementary and Secondary Education Act (ESEA), and the National Science Foundation. Also, Title IV of ESEA has funded the work of regional laboratories and research and development centers. This federal involvement has had some positive effects on the strategy.

The marketing strategy, since it involves commercial enterprises, usually operates from the profit motive. Those companies interested in the education market begin by conducting consumer or market research. They find out through mailings, consultants, or other means what school districts, schools, and school people want or need to buy. Through these means, they determine which materials or equipment to develop and sell. While this has the strength of being oriented toward the needs of practitioners in the schools, it can have the weakness of not depending upon research which tests the effectiveness of products.

Many companies do conduct "product research," which follows a sequence such as that outlined in Figure 6.2. The major positive influence of federal support of material and equipment development is that the government requires such research where federal funds are involved. What this means is that after a new product is developed, it is tested with appropriate target groups and revised if necessary before it is put on the market. In general, practitioners can be relatively sure that educational products developed by Title IV regional laboratories and research and development centers have had rigorous testing. However, since testing is frequently costly, some commercial companies

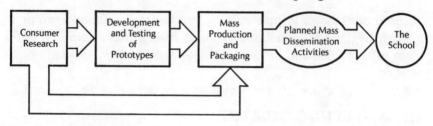

Assumptions	Problems
1 Rational sequence	1 Based on conventional wisdom
2 Planning	2 Over rationality
3 Division of labor	(e.g., inappropriate use)
4 User oriented	3 Inadequate cost-benefit
5 Cost-benefit	ratios in terms of *ultimate* user

FIGURE 6.2   THE MARKETING STRATEGY

prefer to rely only upon the expertise of consultants for development purposes or rely upon making a product attractive and colorful for marketing purposes.

Once a product is developed, it is mass-produced, packaged, and then disseminated to the ultimate target audience, school people. The dissemination occurs through advertising mailouts, ads in popular educational periodicals, presentations in booths at educational conferences, and direct contacts made by salesmen, primarily at the district level. The most serious danger of the marketing strategy is "hucksterism." Commercial firms can capitalize on current trends and fads and couch their claims for success in convincing jargon or pseudoscientific terms.

With the move toward decentralization, which often includes more control over budget at the local school level, it is probable that salesmen will increasingly be knocking on the door of the local school. Because teachers and principals have not been used to buying their own materials, it is possible that monies may be misspent, at least initially. However, there are some aids which school people can rely upon to assist them. For example, Tyler, Klein, and Michael have produced a monograph entitled *Recommendations for Curriculum and Instructional Materials* which sets forth criteria and guidelines for judging the quality of instructional materials.[8] By applying such criteria, or similar ones developed locally, school people can rise above the salesman's rhetoric. At a minimum, when considering the purchase of new products, one should ask, "May I see your field test results?" If there are none, the product may be questionable.

In the past, many instructional materials have been developed for teachers by district personnel, supervisors, and coordinators. Some of these have been of extremely high quality. On the other .hand, the existence of shelves full of dusty district guides and worksheets has become one of the standard jokes of schooling. With high-quality commercial materials from which to select, it does seem somewhat wasteful of talent to have district personnel developing their own curriculum materials. However, pulling together materials, placing them in proper sequences, adapting, and assisting teachers with appropriate use are worthwhile activities for district personnel.

Although the purchase of educational equipment increased markedly during the sixties, the Commission on Instructional Technology reports that much equipment, such as projectors and closed-circuit television, lies idle because teachers are not adequately trained to use it, and even if they are trained they lack the time to set it up. The Commission research indicates that at most only 5 percent of total instructional time utilizes technologically assisted equipment, including motion pictures, filmstrips, overhead projectors, records, television, and computer-assisted programs.[9] Many educators look upon the addition of technology as a "frill," to be utilized only when basic teaching of the three R's has taken place.

High cost is one major reason for the limited impact of technology upon our schools. In computer-assisted instruction (CAI), for example, the computer terminals and the central programming base are extremely expensive. In addition, for both educational television and CAI, the developmental costs for software are high. The Education Development Corporation made an outlay of $6.5 million for one high school physics course. Children's Television Workshop spent $8 million for 130 one-hour television programs.[10] The high cost of developing quality programs means that few are available for school people to use. Another problem is that many people feel that reliance upon equipment and materials is "depersonalizing." A 1969 Harris Poll conducted for *Life* magazine showed that high school students thought CAI and films too passive a way to learn; they preferred more involvement in discussion and community activities.[11]

Although other nations seem to conduct schooling without the massive array of materials and equipment found in our schools, it seems doubtful that the schools of the United States will turn away from them as an important adjunct to schooling; nor should they. In a society as affluent as ours, we should be able to expect that our schools will have available to them whatever tools are necessary to the development of quality programs. The questions one must raise are not about quantity. Rather, they are questions of quality and utilization. Where schools can be equipped with quality materials and equipment, where teachers are adequately trained in their use, and where such materials and equipment can be combined with healthy and appropriate human interactions, learning should be enhanced.

THE RESEARCH, DEVELOPMENT, AND DIFFUSION STRATEGY

The research, development, and diffusion strategy (R, D & D) is based upon the assumption that change should be an orderly process consisting of a rational sequence of activities. It also assumes that there must be extensive planning and division of labor in the change process, and that the ultimate users or targets of the innovation which results from the strategy—school people—are relatively passive and accepting.

Research is the first activity involved in this strategy and is usually, but not necessarily, university-based. Few school districts, state departments of education, or intermediate educational agencies support research efforts beyond the collection of demographic data or routine test results. The federal government supports much educational research through grants to universities, colleges, individuals, and agencies indirectly related to schools (e.g., departments of mental health, community action programs, or art associations). Also, federal research monies come from a variety of sources such as the Department of Labor, the National Institute of Mental Health, the National Science Foundation, the Department of Housing and Urban Development, and the Department of the Interior.[12] Since the mid-sixties the United States Office of Education has directly supported educational research through Title IV of ESEA which established both regional research and development laboratories and university-based research and development centers. Enterprising schools or school districts frequently can take advantage of money thus allocated by serving as subjects for research. Title IV also established the Educational Research Information Centers (ERIC), which disseminate research findings nationwide. All school districts should subscribe to the ERIC system to keep up-to-date.

Development is the second activity involved in the R, D & D strategy. It involves the translation of research findings into some kind of invention which theoretically will improve the program of the ultimate user or target population—the schools. It also includes the field testing of prototypes of new programs. It is here that schools can really benefit from this strategy since programs which need field testing must enter the schools. A school which has identified a particular problem or need can search around for research and development agencies which need to test their products. For example, a school staff which feels it is not adequately teaching critical thinking skills might check pertinent developmental programs in R&D centers, regional laboratories, or universities. By allowing agencies such as the Far West Regional Laboratory, the State University of New York, or a recognized publisher to conduct development activities in the school, that school might improve the critical thinking skills of its students.

As with research activities, funds are available for development activities. Many foundations support such endeavors on behalf of schools,[13] though there is a great deal of competition for such monies. We believe that every school in the nation should be involved in at least one developmental project sponsored by some outside agency related to some identified need or problem. In Appendix A we set forth some guidelines for those who are interested in seeking funds.

Diffusion, the third activity of the R, D & D change strategy, includes both the demonstration of new programs and the dissemination of information about them. Schools which are demonstrating educational innovations should be accessible to potential adopters. In addition, it is important that they be willing to set forth all aspects of the innovation, both positive and negative. Too frequently, other schools find themselves attempting to adopt a new program without having been clearly shown what prerequisites such as cost, necessary training, facilities, materials, and the like are really involved.

Guba has set forth a number of additional diffusion activities. He suggests that those responsible for diffusing an innovation can be helpful to practitioners by (1) acting as a consultant; (2) involving the practitioner in the process of problem identification, development, testing, and packaging of the innovation and diffusing it to others; (3) training the practitioner in the use of the innovation; and (4) intervening to the extent of mandating certain behaviors on the part of the practitioners.[14]

Clark and Guba suggest that the final stage of the process in the schools is adoption, which they divide into three subactivities: trial, installation, and institutionalization.[15] During *trial,* the innovation is tested to see if it can be operated successfully and if, in fact, it is getting the results its advocates claim for it. If the trial is successful, then those in the school will want to *install* it as part of the ongoing program. Finally, it must become *institutionalized,* that is, accepted by all those concerned—teachers, parents, students. At this point, the change process is complete.

The strength of the R, D & D strategy is its high degree of rationality, though none of the advocates of the strategy suggest that all steps must be performed. For example, research may not be necessary in the case of an already proven innovation such as team teaching. The critical point is that the strategy sets forth a logical sequence of activities. If such a sequence is followed, there is at least the chance that problems can be foreseen and worked through prior to their actually arising.

On the other hand, the very strength of the strategy may well be its greatest weakness. Inherent in a rational sequence of activities is the division of labor. Thus, the strategy requires, especially in regard to diffusion activities, that researchers based in universities, laboratories, and research centers work closely with practitioners. However, often these researchers have only the vaguest of notions about what the operations and problems of the school are really like. Similarly, the practitioner frequently lacks an understanding of or even holds a disdain for research and the researcher. Further, each group often has its own vested interests. The researcher may be preoccupied with writing scholarly research papers while the practitioner must meet the daily demands of "keeping school." Often there is little time left for fruitful discourse and collaboration.

The R, D & D strategy is, in general, the strategy utilized by the federal government with regard to education. Title IV of ESEA established federally supported research centers and laboratories for development work. The work of these centers is now supported by the National Institute of Education (NIE). Under Title III, supplementary centers were funded to perform diffusion activities. At present, however, Title III has been almost totally turned over to the states to operate and in only a few states, such as New York, Pennsylvania, North Carolina, and Texas, does any semblance of the Title III supplementary centers still perform the diffusion function. It can only be hoped that our educational agencies will not overlook 'diffusion as a very important aspect of change.

THE CHANGE-AGENT STRATEGY

Some school systems and many intermediate educational agencies, recognizing the importance of bridging the theory-practice gap, are beginning to employ people specifically to act as change agents in schools. While such people may hold a variety of titles, their main tasks are to act as catalysts, agitators, questioners, trainers, and creators of awareness of change.

Several authors have written about the role of the change agent. Jung, for example, listed the following functions of the change agent within the school system:

> He relates to staffs or schools and to central administrators in identifying needs for providing training.
>
> He provides demonstration of some skills.
>
> He trains staff in some skills.
>
> He makes support for training available (e.g., clerical help, released time).
>
> He arranges staff access to other training resources (e.g., brings in trainers from outside for internal events, arranges involvement in outside training activities, provides materials for self-training).
>
> He works to coordinate administration, research, and training as an integrated part of the system's problem-solving procedures.[16]

Havelock suggested that there are three primary ways in which a person can act as a change agent. These are as a catalyst, as a solution giver, or as a process helper.[17] The catalyst is a person who prods and pressures the system to overcome its inertia. The solution giver provides answers to specific questions or problems faced by the school. The process helper assists people with the various stages of problem solving.

In general, those who write about "change agentry" suggest two types of analyses that the change agent should make of the client population: the kind of people he will be dealing with and the stages of change through which people go.

In analyzing the people who make up an organization in order to make changes in that organization, one can usually identify three critical targets. There are (1) the early adopters, (2) the resisters, and (3) the leaders. In almost every school there are staff members who are open to change and willing to try new things. They are the innovators or *early adopters*. The change agent should identify these people early and begin to solicit their support. While early adopters may vary from innovation to innovation, it is generally true that they tend to be more open-minded and to look outward for new ideas.

A second group which is relatively easy to identify is the *resisters*. It is dangerous to generalize about resistance, for people may resist changes for very different reasons and a person who resists one change may not necessarily resist another. Some people may resist because an innovation somehow impinges upon their personal values. Teachers or parents who value history, for example, might resist a new social studies program which is based upon concepts and generalizations derived from the behavioral sciences or economic geography.[18] Other people are simply uninformed about alternative ways of doing things. The change agent must make sure that appropriate information or experiences are provided for such people. Any innovation which is to be considered for adoption by a school system should be introduced through a well-planned in-service program for staff, and through informative public relations sessions with board members and parents. There are, also, of course, people so alienated from a system that they will resist almost any innovation. In such cases there are usually other underlying causes not related to the innovation itself. These causes, too, must be dealt with to prevent resistance from being used as a weapon against the system.

People can find all kinds of reasons for not adopting a new practice. In such cases, the change agent must carefully analyze the purported reasons for resistance and plan specific strategies for dealing with them. He can demonstrate new methods; he can clarify regulations when they are thought to be in the way of adopting a new practice; he can reinforce those who are anxious to move ahead by allowing them freedom of trial; or he can help people see why past trials might have failed.

Finally, there are *leaders*—formal and informal—among the staff members. Department heads, team leaders, grade-level chairmen, project coordinators, counselors, and the like are formal leaders. Their support of changes is essential. Also, there are informal leaders whose opinions are often highly regarded by members of the staff. Their support, too, should be solicited.

As discussed in Chapter 5, people tend to go through stages of behavior which ultimately lead them to the adoption of an innovation. As Rogers[19] points out, initially, people become aware of a new idea. The change agent can create such awareness or promote it with an article, book, film, or speaker. When an individual or group moves from awareness to active interest and information seeking, then the change agent can provide more information. At this stage, a teacher from another school where the idea has been utilized can be a valuable resource. Once people have gathered sufficient information, they begin in their minds to evaluate the utility of the new idea for themselves. It is at this point that visits to successful programs nearby can be of most value. It is also advisable to have people visit schools similar to their own where the innovation is being practiced. Often, when people visit schools that are unique (e.g., outstanding facilities, outstanding teachers, extra equipment, unique students), they get the feeling that the new idea won't work "back home."

If an idea has been evaluated and found to be worthwhile, people will want to test it. It is at this point that the change agent must provide appropriate in-service training using appropriate resource personnel. Then, after an innovation has been adopted and integrated into the ongoing program, the change agent will continue to assist by providing necessary services such as time, space, materials, and personnel. He will also give encouragement and serve as a transactional agent, translating the new program to parents, the district, and other staff members.

Such stages, while not rigidly prescribed, are important. Most change efforts that fail, and these are countless, result from efforts to try something new without consideration of the human necessity to become interested, to evaluate, and simply to have time to adjust.

Typically, the change agent is thought of as someone outside the system. He may come from a university, a county office, a supplementary center, or from any number of other external agencies. However, there are not enough of these external change agents to meet the needs of all of the schools in the nation. Thus, it becomes important that each school district and individual school develop the talents of those incumbents who could perform the change-agent role. The principal is critical, of course, as are team leaders, department heads, counselors, resource teachers of various kinds, grade level chairmen, or chairmen of parent workshops. All such people, because they perform leadership roles in the school, can be change agents. Likewise, at the district level, coordinators, supervisors, psychologists, directors, and various other specialists can be change agents.

Viewing people in incumbent positions as change agents has its problems, for as we said in discussing authority and influence, such incumbents often see themselves and are trained as givers of knowledge rather than process facilitators whose objective is to build independence and self-renewing capabilities in their schools. On the other hand, choosing people from existing staff and retraining them as change agents makes good sense. School budgets are continually being scrutinized and even cut, so that districts often can no longer afford the luxury of numerous coordinators and supervisors. What they can afford is a small cadre of highly trained change agents who can work with teachers and others to improve the schools.

THE PROBLEM-SOLVING STRATEGY

The use of authority, marketing, and the R, D & D strategies all view the school as a recipient of knowledge produced by others; the change-agent strategy concentrates on linking the school to knowledge from the outside. Those who advocate problem solving as a change strategy move even further toward the school as the critical unit of change. The rationale for this strategy is based upon the assumption that self-initiated change in a school has the best chance of success because the staff is highly motivated to make it work. The strategy assumes that staff members, either alone or with the assistance of outside change agents, go through a series of behaviors which ultimately lead them both to problem solution and to what is referred to in the literature as "self-renewing" behavior.[20] Self-renewal means that once a school staff learns problem-solving behavior, it will continue this behavior as new problems arise.

In general, the problem-solving strategy stems from Lewin's concept of three stages of change: unfreezing, moving, and freezing.[21] In the *unfreezing* stage the school becomes aware of a problem. There is disagreement over whether the initiation of problem awareness should come from within the school or from an outside source. The slowness of inside initiation and the need for specialized "process" skills are arguments for an outside agent. Those who argue for internal initiation first suggest that there are not enough change agents to go around and second emphasize the ultimate importance of the practitioner identifying his own problems. Regardless of whether or not an outside agent is used, it is critical that the staff be aware of and committed to the need to solve the problem.

After unfreezing, the next stage is *moving*. There are many problem-solving cycles, each with its own steps. Figure 6.3 describes an example of a model developed from Lewin's work. First, after a clear and concise statement of what the problem is, the problem is *analyzed*. Factors which bear upon the problem are identified by asking: What factors cause the problem? How can the problem be alleviated? Can this problem be subdivided into more manageable problems? Is this problem

FIGURE 6.3 PROBLEM-SOLVING CONSTRUCT

This model was first developed by Jerrold M. Novotney and is presented in *The Dynamics of Educational Leadership,* Educational Resource Associates, Inc., Los Angeles, California, 1973.

related to other problems? Problem analysis is a diagnostic step in the sense that an attempt is made to determine the nature of the forces or circumstances affecting the present state. Then it becomes easier to set priorities for attacking the various circumstances. The results of the analysis should be the pinpointing of elements of the problem which hold potential as alternative solutions.

Once the analysis is completed, an *objective* is set which will solve or remove the problem. The question that must be asked is, "Do we have the right objective?"

Then an *inventory* of resources should be made including both material and human resources. For material resources, it is useful to chart the availability of each, together with an estimate of its utility in relation to the objective. In dealing with human resources, a list should be made of what the various people in the organization (or those available to it) can do to assist in reaching the objective.

Organization refers to the development of a plan which will allow the objective to be reached. The three necessary ingredients of such a plan are: (1) a chronological sequence of activities, (2) the points at which resources need to be introduced, and (3) the time required for each task. An *operational* push may come in the form of group consensus to act, an oral command, a written memo, or a powerful leadership act; it signals the group's willingness to accept its responsibility. This is the point at which things actually begin to happen and the movement toward problem solution is begun.

There must be two types of *evaluation*. First, how well is the group moving through the problem-solving process? Perhaps the process isn't working (e.g., an adequate analysis or inventory is not made or the objective is not clearly related to the problem). This "process" evaluation occurs throughout the problem-solving cycle. Second, at the end of the process we need to know how well we met the objective. Therefore, in order to conduct "terminal" evaluation, one must set criteria against which success is measured. Also, ways of measuring (e.g., questionnaires, standardized measures, interviews) should be specified and means of collecting data set forth.

Where the evaluation process points up an obstacle or a deficiency, a review of the previous steps is in order. Due to miscalculation or erroneous data, alteration may have to be made in the analysis of the problem, statement of objectives, inventory of resources, organization, or operation. Once the evaluation feedback has been used to redirect efforts, the process is begun again.

The final stage of change described by Lewin is *freezing*. In short, this means that when a change has been brought about, it has to become somehow a stable part of the ongoing program. Frequently, changes disappear after change efforts cease, and the system reverts to its old ways of operating. This is particularly true in a situation where the change has been dependent primarily upon the efforts of an external change agent or even upon a single person within the system, such as the principal. Thus, it is critical to have a broad base of active support for a change.

One program which has been developed for use by school staffs without reliance upon an external change agent is the *Problem Solving School* (PSS). Designed for elementary schools, the PSS Program consists of a two-part set of programmed materials and exercises. One part focuses on the problems of individual teachers or teaching teams, and the other deals with problems that usually affect everyone in the school. For problems affecting the total staff, the kit includes teacher guides, a principal's guide, and assignment sheets to help teachers strengthen problem-solving skills in large and small group meetings. The guidelines aid in effective planning and structuring of meetings, the identification of problems, the search for solutions, and the implementation and evaluation of alternatives. For problems encountered in teaching, a separate series of five booklets helps the teacher learn or review useful skills, suggests ways to practice these skills, and provides guides for trading ideas in small group sessions.[22]

All the strategies for change discussed in this chapter—the use of authority and influence; marketing; research, development, and diffusion; utilizing a change agent; and problem solving—are well researched and proven strategies. If they are understood and carefully applied singly or in combination in a school, they can bring about lasting improvements in the school program. In addition, because of recent efforts to improve our schools, we are beginning to see the emergence of a number of newer strategies which, while they have not been totally proven, hold promise for the years to come. It it these emerging strategies which we shall examine in Chapter 7.

NOTES

1 Kenneth A. Tye, "Creating Impact," U.S. Office of Education, Bureau of Elementary and Secondary Education, Division of Plans and Supplementary Centers, Washington, D.C., 1967. (Mimeographed.)

2 Morris Janowitz, *Institution Building in Urban Education*, Russell Sage Foundation, Connecticut Printers, Inc., Hartford, 1969, p. 20.

3 John P. French and Bertram H. Raven, "The Bases of Social Power," in Dorwin Cartwright (ed.), *Studies in Social Power*, University of Michigan Institute for Social Research, Research Center for Group Dynamics, 1959.

4 See Stephen K. Bailey, "Teachers' Centres: A British First," *Phi Delta Kappan,* November 1971, pp. 146–149.

5 Association of California School Administrators, *Project Leadership— What Can It Do?*, Association of California School Administrators, Project Leadership, Irvine, Calif., 1970.

6 Douglas McGregor, *The Human Side of Enterprise*, McGraw-Hill, New York, 1960.

7 This application of McGregor's X-Y theory to schools appeared previously in John I. Goodlad, M. Frances Klein, Jerrold M. Novotney, Kenneth A. Tye, and Associates, *Toward a Mankind School: An Adventure in Humanistic Education*, McGraw-Hill, New York, 1974, p. 22.

8   Louise L. Tyler, M. Frances Klein, and William B. Michael, *Recommendations for Curriculum and Instructional Materials,* Tyl Press, Los Angeles, 1971; rev. ed., Educational Resource Associates, Los Angeles, 1976.

9   U.S. Commission on Instructional Technology, *To Improve Learning,* House of Representatives, Committee on Education and Labor, Washington, D.C., March 1970.

10 Ibid.

11 Louis Harris and Associates, Inc., "The *Life* Poll: Crisis in the High Schools," *Life,* vol. 66, no. 19, p. 30, May 16, 1969.

12 A good sourcebook for federal grants to educational research and other educational projects is U.S. Office of Management and Budget, *1974 Catalog of Federal Domestic Assistance,* Washington, D.C., 1974. Updated annually.

13 There are several directories which describe foundation interests, assets, projects funded, etc. One good source is *Foundation Profiles,* Taft Products, Inc., Washington, D.C., 1973.

14 Egon G. Guba, "Development, Diffusion and Evaluation," in T. L. Eidell and Joanne M. Ketchel (eds.), *Knowledge, Production and Utilization in Educational Administration,* University of Oregon, Center for Advanced Study of Educational Administration, Eugene, 1968.

15 David Clark and Egon Guba, "An Examination of Potential Change Roles," paper presented at the Symposium on Innovation in Planning School Curricula, Airlee House, Va., October 1965.

16 Charles C. Jung, "The Trainer Change-Agent Role within a School System," in Goodwin Watson (ed.), *Change in School Systems,* National Education Association, National Training Laboratory, Washington, D.C., 1967, p. 103.

17 Ronald G. Havelock, *Guide to Innovation in Education,* Center for Research on Utilization of Scientific Knowledge, Institute for Social Research, University of Michigan, Ann Arbor, 1970. This book, written for practitioners, is a valuable guide to those who wish to be change agents.

18 Gerhard Eicholz presents a framework for the identification of forms of rejection of new ideas. He points out that people may be uninformed, doubtful, comparing, defensive, anxious, alienated, or otherwise disposed. See Gerhard C. Eicholz, "Why Do Teachers Reject Change?" *Theory into Practice,* vol. 2, pp. 264–268, December 1963.

19 Adapted from Everett M. Rogers, *Diffusion of Innovation,* Free Press, New York, 1969.

20   See, for example, Matthew Miles and Dale Lake, "Self-Renewal in School Systems: A Strategy for Planned Change," in Goodwin Watson (ed.), *Concepts for Social Change,* National Training Laboratory, Institute for Applied Behavioral Science, Washington, D.C., 1967; and Richard Schmuck, Philip J. Runkel, and Daniel Langmeyer, "Improving Organizational Problem Solving in a School Faculty," *Applied Behavioral Science,* vol. 5, no. 4, October/November/December 1969.

21   Kurt Lewin, "Group Decision and Social Change," in Guy E. Swanson et al. (eds.), *Readings in Social Psychology,* Henry Holt and Company, New York, 1952.

22   *The Problem Solving School Program Kit* is available from the Institute for Development of Educational Activities, Inc. (|I|D|E|A|), Information and Services Division, P.O. Box 446, Melbourne, Florida 32901.

CHAPTER 7

FUTURE CHANGE STRATEGIES

Contemporary literature gives many clues on bringing about educational change in the future. This literature contains such new terms as planning-programming-budgeting systems (PPBS), guaranteed performance contracting, teacher power, home television, cassette learning, free schools, student power, self-help, integrated day, franchise schools, "age span" programs, systems planning, voucher plans, community involvement, experimental networks, internships, decentralization, alternative schools, cybernetics, synergistics, behavior modification, and leagues of schools. All these terms, as varied as they are, have at least two things in common. First, they have resulted, in one way or another, from our basic concerns in the mid-sixties for quality education and equality of educational opportunity. Second, they all hold some promise for bringing about change in American schooling.

None of the ideas set out above represents a change strategy per se. Collectively, however, they give hints as to how our schools may be changed in the years to come. The problem is to mold such promising ideas into meaningful and workable strategies which will bring about quality education and equality of educational opportunity.

Emerging ideas related to changing American education can be arbitrarily grouped into a number of broad categories: (1) personnel strategies, (2) scientific management, (3) alternative education, (4) political strategies, and (5) peer-support strategies.

PERSONNEL STRATEGIES

Education is a human endeavor. Nearly 80 percent of all operating funds (exclusive of capital outlay) go to the payment of salaries and benefits for people. Further, despite all efforts to make instruction "teacher free," the cornerstone of schooling is ultimately the kind and quality of interactions among students and adults in the school.

In one way or another, the importance of the human dimension of schooling has always been recognized. Pre-service training of teachers, for example, has been extended from a one-year normal school program to a four-year program including a bachelor of arts, science, or education degree. In some states such training has even been extended to five years. In-service training programs for teachers and administrators have been developed and implemented in nearly every school district in the nation. Salary increases, more often than not, are closely related to advanced training at colleges and universities. At the national level, National Defense Education Act (NDEA) and National Science Foundation (NSF) Institutes have been designed to update teachers and to familiarize them with new methods and content. Finally, the Educational Professional Development Act (EPDA) and Titles I and II ESEA funds have spurred in-service training activities, particularly for teachers in the nation's inner-city schools.

Even with such efforts, however, the development of improved personnel has not kept pace with the changing needs of America's schools. To be sure, upgrading the knowledge, skills, and abilities of school personnel is only a partial answer to the problems faced by our schools. However, it is important, and because of this importance, comprehensive strategies need to be designed and implemented. In general, such strategies need to consider at least three dimensions: (1) the differentiation of roles, (2) the organization of schools for staff development programs, and (3) the recruitment of people with differing social backgrounds into the field.

Role Differentiation

Few people would tolerate a lengthy stay as a patient in a hospital in which a doctor was responsible for planning the hospital budget, billing and collecting from thirty-six patients, serving meals, carrying bedpans, making beds, and finally, diagnosing and prescribing for patients. We have come to expect that the doctor will perform only his truly professional role—that of diagnostician and prescriber. Other tasks which keep the hospital operational are performed by administrators, nurses, interns, student nurses, orderlies, and even volunteer aids.

The comparison to schools is obvious and it has been made many times before. The teacher, like the doctor, should be responsible for truly professional behavior—that of diagnosing, prescribing, and establishing an atmosphere wherein quality instruction and learning can take place. Tasks such as collecting milk or picture money, keeping attendance records, setting up materials for art lessons, or putting up bulletin boards can and should be carried out by others. Again like the medical profession, further specialization is required. Just as there is need for the internist, dermatologist, and bone specialist, there is also the need for the teacher with special skills in perception, inquiry training, and psychological reinforcement.

There is much movement in the direction of differentiating among roles to be played in our schools. One plan which has been well publicized and which has been supported experimentally with EPDA funds has been differentiated staffing.[1] Differentiated staffing plans operate from the assumptions that teachers are becoming increasingly more competent, that they should receive appropriate remuneration for such competence, and that the so-called single salary schedule must go if such competence is to be rewarded adequately.

Under such a plan there can be curriculum development and research specialists, senior teachers, staff teachers, associate teachers, interns, and paraprofessionals. The categories and their hierarchical ranking will depend on need and will differ from site to site. The essential point is that differentiated staffing provides for increased autonomy and decision-making power for teachers and offers a chance for competency-based advancement and an opportunity for some type of professionally based peer evaluation system.

Differentiated staffing patterns, while they exist in a number of schools, have failed to become common practice largely because of the cost of installation. However, the use of teacher-aids, parent volunteers, interns, and even older students as aids has become fairly common in the schools of America. There is no one plan which will suit all the schools of the nation. However, the principle that we need to differentiate roles within our schools and the principle that teacher competencies need to be utilized to their fullest cannot be denied. Perhaps the strategy best employed is to adopt such principles and then to let each school develop its own differentiation plan commensurate with its needs and resources.[2] It is through plans such as this that we may be able to overcome some of our common expectations which tend to impede educational change (e.g., thirty children equal one teacher).

There is one danger which is to be avoided in differentiated staff programs. It arises from the concern set forth in Chapter 3 regarding formalization and, particularly, stratification in an organization. That is, if differentiation of roles leads to hard-and-fast delineation of duties or if salaries are significantly differentiated among roles, the rate of change may be slowed. To avoid such dangers, differentiated staffing plans must also build collegial decision-making structures (see Chapter 3 regarding decision making) and must build reward systems based upon intrinsic factors such as trust, job satisfaction, appreciation, and participation rather than upon extrinsic financial rewards which tend to separate people from the acceptance of common goals.

Organizing Schools for Staff Development

The notion that effective in-service training can take place on Thursday afternoon after school is a poor one at best. Teachers themselves are recognizing this, and union and association contract negotiators are beginning to demand either time off or extra pay for teachers involved in in-service training activities.

Another poor notion about in-service training is encouraged by present salary schedules. Individual teachers are rewarded for going off to a college, university, or extension program and taking course work to improve themselves. The result is that many are working toward a degree in school administration or psychometrics, work which may have little bearing upon their work in the classroom. While the salary rewards may be there for the teacher, whether there are rewards to the students in the form of improved teaching is problematic.

There are trends in staff development which seem to hold promise for the future. First, more and more districts are recognizing the fact that there must be time set aside for staff development activities. The Unity School District in Maine had to cut the school week to four days for financial reasons. At the end of the school year, the district found that there were no significant differences in terms of student achievement. As a result, after funds were restored, the district decided to continue on a four-day instructional schedule with the fifth day set aside for staff development. A study by the Maine State Department of Education showed that parents, while originally skeptical, have come to support the program.[3]

Not all school districts will be able to have teachers and others involved with staff development activities for one full day a week. However, there are many arrangements short of this which can be made. There can be early dismissals on a certain number of days per year, month, or week. There can be weekend or summer workshops with staff members paid for time worked. There can be differentiated staffing arrangements with various people free during the day for in-service activities. Finally, programs such as the year-round school offer great flexibility to staffs in terms of planned staff development activities.

A second encouraging trend is that teacher-training institutions are beginning to recognize the need to combine their pre-service training activities with in-service training. This trend arises out of the recognition of the need for closer working relationships with practitioners in the field and because of an emerging oversupply of teachers. The combination of in-service and pre-service training programs can take many forms. One of note is the program of the Teacher Education Laboratory at UCLA. Rather than the usual pattern of assigning a prospective teacher to a master teacher in some nearby school, a group of prospective teachers is assigned to a school, department, or teaching team. Personnel from the Laboratory also are assigned to the school, department, or team with the task of working with *all* the teachers, not just the student teachers. Also, Laboratory personnel can move from school to school utilizing their specific talents. They, too, are a team. To back up its work in the field, the Teacher Education Laboratory has also developed or purchased instructional tape, filmstrip, slide, and written "modules" which can be used by pre- and in-service teachers on such varied topics as inquiry training, setting behavioral objectives, and techniques for teaching reading.

Perhaps the most encouraging trend in terms of staff development is the move toward total school or at least team or department staff-development programs. Some of these activities focus on organizational development (OD) dimensions (e.g., interpersonal communications, problem solving) while others are less "process" and more "content" oriented. The strength of this movement resides in its focus upon "real" school problems and in its overcoming the notion that schooling can be improved through each individual going off to take his own course work.

Recruitment of People with Differing Social Values

It is a fact that most of today's teachers are members of the white middle class, a group whose conservative tendencies may inhibit change. To counteract such a situation, a concerted effort should be made to recruit new social types into teaching. By "new social types" we mean representatives of minority groups, the young—and old—who are committed to social change, and representatives of all social and economic classes. No longer can we view our schools as havens for young middle-class women who are biding their time until marriage, or for middle-aged middle-class women motivated primarily by the need to supplement the family income. Neither can we afford to choose our leadership only from those who have "survived" in the system for a decade or two, for survivorship is frequently synonymous with maintenance of the status quo. No doubt there are many middle-class women, young and old, who can make a contribution to our schools; and no doubt there are those who have been in the system for some time who will be good leaders. But the point remains that we need a broader range of people staffing our schools.

Beyond improved pre-service and in-service training programs, there is a need to alter the criteria used to select persons who are to fill the various positions in our schools. Typically, criteria such as appearance, voice, health, training, courses taken, and "philosophy" (a nebulous criterion at best) are used to make decisions about who should or should not be employed. Some school districts, recognizing the inadequacy of such criteria, are beginning to develop more appropriate ones. For example, in Anaheim, California, potential teachers must demonstrate knowledge of new ideas in schooling. Further, candidates must demonstrate an awareness of what needs to be improved in schooling. "Awareness" is tested through a series of questions, such as, "If you could, how would you improve your student teaching experience?" Finally, teachers who supervise student teachers are receiving special training in appraising and in writing appraisals of potential teachers.

One recruitment problem which faces our schools in the seventies, and which will probably exist for some time to come, is that of an oversupply of teachers. The oversupply can be viewed as an advantage in terms of having a larger population from which to select. On the other hand, because of intense competition for jobs, those holding positions are not apt to be as mobile as they have been in the past. Teachers will be less apt to resign for maternity or other reasons because their reentry into jobs will not be as easy as it has been in the past. Thus, the oversupply of teachers is causing people to sit tight in their positions. When incumbents tend to stay in their positions and when, as in most states, there are strong tenure laws, it becomes very difficult—if not impossible—to recruit new, more change-oriented people into the field.

Some states, recognizing the limitations now placed upon recruitment, are directly assaulting existing tenure laws or, as in New Mexico, are calling for periodic recertification for teachers. While the battle over tenure may result in some changes in recruitment, it runs the very high risk of having a negative effect upon educational change in that it raises a sensitive and highly political issue which could split the profession itself.

A somewhat less sensitive and perhaps more promising attack upon the problem of recruitment may reside in the arena of voluntary early retirement, now being tested in Pasadena, California. Most states have retirement laws which allow or force teachers and administrators to retire in their sixties. If districts could give incentives to allow people to retire in their fifties, they could gain considerable flexibility in bringing younger, more change-oriented people into the schools. Such incentives would, by and large, have to be in the form of higher retirement pay. The argument that this would be too costly is not necessarily true. Personal contributions could be increased and part-time teaching arrangements could supplement retirement income. Also, by decreasing the average age of the teaching force, the average salary level of teachers should be decreased correspondingly. The major advantage of exploring early retirement—aside from its low cost and its obvious opening up of recruitment options—is that it is a concept being explored in other industries and institutions and thus has some public appeal.

SCIENTIFIC MANAGEMENT

Many schools are being faced with the task of being more "accountable" for their results. Simply stated, this means that they must show, usually through test results, that students are achieving at or above some agreed upon predetermined level. The performance of teachers and others will be evaluated on the basis of such results. Related to the idea of accountability are a whole set of planning and budgeting techniques including systems planning and PPBS. Finally, there is the behavioral objectives movement which calls for teachers to state intended pupil outcomes in specific behavioral terms, for administrators to "manage by objectives," and for teachers to be evaluated on the basis of their performance. Such terms—accountability, performance evaluation, systems planning, PPBS, guaranteed performance contracting—all are part of a movement to make the management of education more "scientific," a movement which dates back to the 1920s.[4]

Accountability

Ewald Nyquist has defined accountability as follows:

> Accountability means to me a continuous willingness to evaluate education, to explain and interpret the results with all candor, to divulge the results to the publics or constituencies that need to know them, and to be personally and organizationally responsible for the weaknesses as well as the strengths revealed. . . . what it means is that school boards and local and state educators will face the responsibility of taking the public into full partnership—explaining the problems and limitations of testing and other means of evaluating education, welcoming assistance, and sharing the resulting information (after having done everything possible to assure that it will be properly interpreted and used).[5]

Cornell sees accountability as a process having four components:

1   Specification of desired learner performance.
2   Specification of those processes which will be implemented in order to bring about the desired learner performance.
3   Establishment of procedures to monitor and audit the above processes to determine if they are in fact implemented.
4   Publication of a report relating student performance to the implemented educational program.[6]

There are significant problems connected with the trend toward accountability in education. First, despite protestations to the contrary, accountability systems can appear, as Seldin says, to make teachers the "scapegoats" for all the problems and failures of American education.[7] The fact is that education is a complex enterprise and few, if any, advocates of accountability are discussing the roles of legislators, boards of education, district administrators, or the public.

Second, there has been little clarification of what the schools must be accountable for. The use of standardized tests or even criterion-referenced measures in skill and content areas to determine accountability leaves a great deal to be desired for those interested in more humanistic goals of schooling. Also, despite the rhetoric and the promises made by proponents, accountability systems are imposed systems, and one must wonder if they will lead to self-renewing schools and teachers.

Performance Evaluation

An outgrowth of the accountability movement is the idea that all personnel in the school should be evaluated on the basis of their actual performance. For example, as a result of the Stull Bill passed by the California Legislature, each principal—or his representative—has to meet with each probationary teacher and half of the tenured teachers by October 15. At that meeting, and subsequent ones for other teachers, mutually agreed upon specific behavioral objectives for the students under the charge of each teacher were established. The attainment or nonattainment of these objectives, as measured each spring, was to serve as the "scientific" basis for evaluating the teacher's performance.

If we assume that students are products, then perhaps we can use test results to determine who is a good teacher. On the other hand, if we are concerned with the kinds of people students are becoming, then we likewise want to be concerned with what kind of person the teacher is, what methods he or she uses, and what models he or she presents. It may be all right to measure a salesman's productivity on the basis of the number of his sales, a rancher's productivity on the basis of how large his steers are at market time, or an assembly-line worker's productivity on the basis of how many pieces he turns out. These are performance questions. But when and how do we ask about the built-in obsolescence in the goods we buy, the alarming growth of cholesterol problems in our society, or the mechanical failures built into many of the products which come from our factories?

It may be that performance evaluation will help us improve our schools. But one still must wonder about those things we have difficulty in measuring: humaneness, creativity, independence of spirit, love of life, appreciation of beauty, dedication to our fellow beings, and the improvement of the human condition through inquiry and rational problem solving. Right now, performance evaluation seems to be dealing with quantitative matters only. We also need to be concerned with quality.

Systems Planning and Program Budgeting

As part of the current scientific management movement, many people in education are moving to forms of systems planning. Such planning generally takes an educational planner through a series of steps which gives the institution a "direction" for achieving its goals. The process can be simple or complex. Bentzen and Tye summarize:

There are . . . modes of planning and analysis which can be utilized to make more rational decisions about efficient use of resources (inputs) in order to gain maximum educational benefits (outputs). These newer modes, such as cost-benefit analysis, systems analysis, and program budgeting, have been utilized successfully by many government agencies to make budgetary decisions. In general, these modes involve the following steps: (a) identification of objectives, (b) identification of alternative programs, (c) estimation of costs and resources necessary to each alternative, (d) development of . . . models which define relationships between inputs and outputs, (e) identification of performance criteria, (f) making decisions based on the application of criteria to alternative programs, and (g) measurement of the attainment of objectives. At the same time, such procedures must be followed with caution lest they become a mere mystique. They have no inherent merit superior to the values of the persons who utilize them.[8]

A major problem with systems planning and PPBS is that they are often imposed, moving downward from the state level to the districts and then to schools. There is the very real danger that such systems will do more to rigidify operations than to create an open climate in which change can occur. It is interesting to note that while many governmental and school agencies are moving toward more structured management systems, many businesses and industries are moving toward participatory management.

There is also a very real problem in applying cost-benefit procedures to some areas of human behavior. As with performance evaluation, one must raise the question of goals. Similarly, while we may be able to deal with quantitative questions, we still are ill-equipped to deal with questions of values and quality of life. Even with the use of highly sophisticated computers, we cannot avoid the necessity of employing human judgment. And it is here that "systems" can break down.

On the other side of the ledger, systematic planning does hold promise for schools interested in change. To begin with, such planning frequently calls for teachers and community members to be deeply involved in assessing the needs of their schools and in setting goals for their schools. For another, it enables schools to make cost/benefit analyses of their program. Generally, educational expenditures are reported as line items under a dozen or more broad headings, including such things as instruction, administration, transportation, and capital outlay. Under this system, there is absolutely no way to determine how much a given program such as art, reading, social studies, or language arts costs; and, obviously, there is no way of relating costs to benefits gained. Program budgeting could provide such information, enabling decisions about the value of programs to be made.

Guaranteed Performance Contracting

As a change strategy, guaranteed performance contracting proposes to create alternatives, innovation, and change within the school system by means of outside intervention or management.

According to Lessinger, a performance contract is a legal agreement between a local school board and a supplier of instructional programs.[9] Payment to the supplier or firm depends on the degree of student improvement, which is independently audited or evaluated. More specifically, performance contracting is a formal agreement between a local board of education and a contractor "to achieve certain specified gains in student performance within a specified period of time." Payment is based upon results.[10]

Generally, performance contracts have been agreements between school boards and private business (e.g., Dorsett Educational Systems and Texarkana, Arkansas; Westinghouse Learning Corporation and Gilroy, California). The focus is upon the quantitative measurement of pupil achievement, with the contract identifying specific objectives ("Each student assigned to the center will have an objective of achieving not less than 1.0 achievement years in reading and math . . ."). By and large, the target population has been disadvantaged groups or students of low-income families, and payment has come largely from Title I–ESEA funds. Frankly, the movement has not yet spread across the nation because results have been mixed.

In considering the tools of scientific management, the problem is to realize that they are only tools, perhaps even dangerous ones. They stem from two assumptions: first, that the schools are doing poorly, and second, that somehow tools of scientific management which can assist in quantifying outcomes will improve the schools. Schools can do better, no doubt. But better quantification is not necessarily the way to improve the functioning of a complex social system.

ALTERNATIVE EDUCATION

Almost antithetical to the scientific management movement is the movement toward "alternative" education. Where the former derives its impetus from neo-behaviorists, the latter can be said to arise from the works of the neo-humanists such as Holt, Leonard, Glasser, Kohl, Rogers, and Illich.[11]

The term "alternative" education can mean different things to different people and covers a wide variety of possible arrangements. Most of us are familiar with the free school and storefront school, for example, which are generally community-based and operated outside of the public education system. At the other end of the continuum—if there is a continuum—are parochial schools, which, while operating separately from the public schools, most frequently resemble public schools with the addition of some form of religious instruction.

Smith described the various types of alternative schools in operation as:

> *Open Schools*—with learning activities individualized and organized around interest centers within the classroom or building.
>
> *Schools Without Walls*—with learning activities throughout the community and with much interaction between school and community.
>
> *Magnet Schools, Learning Centers, Educational Parks*—with a concentration of learning resources in one center available to all of the students in the community.
>
> *Multicultural Schools, Bilingual Schools, Ethnic Schools*—with emphasis on cultural pluralism and ethnic and racial awareness.
>
> *Street Academies, Dropout Centers, Pregnancy-Maternity Centers*—with emphasis on learning programs for students in targeted populations.
>
> *School-Within-a-School*—could be any of the above organized as a unit within a conventional school.
>
> *Integration Models*—could be any of the above with a voluntary population that is representative in racial, ethnic, and socioeconomic class makeup of the total population of the community.
>
> *Free Schools*—with emphasis on greater freedom for students and teachers. This term is usually applied to nonpublic alternatives, but a very few are operating within public school systems today.[12]

The purpose of such alternative schools is to provide students and parents with more options and choices. They attempt to focus upon a broader array of goals and objectives (e.g., development of self-concept; encouragement of social pluralism; the preparation of students for a variety of social roles such as voter, consumer, and parent). They hope to be more flexible and utilize formative evaluation techniques, and they try to be more humane through personalization and through the elimination of bureaucratic constraints. The under-girding notion, which we have already espoused, is that the single school with its students, staff, and parents is the critical unit in which to bring about educational improvement.

Many of the problems of the so-called alternative movement are caused by those who promote it, who are sometimes overzealous and even simple-minded. They often appear to be demanding that their one alternative be imposed upon the total system, which, of course, flies in the face of the movement's basic notion of choice.

Fantini poses the same problem in a slightly different way and calls it the "psychology of labeling."[13] He points out that the advocates who use words such as "open," "individualized," and "humanistic" are by implication suggesting that only their programs have such characteristics. Not only can this cause resentment, but it can lead to bitter conflict that is less than productive for the schools.

In order to legitimatize alternatives under a public school framework, Fantini suggests application of the following criteria:

1 The alternative must be made available to students, teachers, and parents by choice. It cannot be superimposed.

2 It cannot claim the capacity to replace existing alternatives like the standard school. Premature claims of superiority, belittling the worth of other alternatives, tend to create a negative political climate. The option being advanced is just that: an option for those students, parents and teachers who are *attracted* to it. The existing alternatives are just as legitimate as those being proposed.

3 It must give evidence of being geared to the attainment of a comprehensive set of educational objectives, those for which the public school is accountable and not merely selected ones. . . .

4 It is not designed to promote exclusivity—racial, religious, or socioeconomic. Equal access must be guaranteed.

5 It is not dependent on significant amounts of extra money to implement and does not increase the per-student expenditures beyond those of established options. The idea is to utilize existing resources differently—perhaps more effectively.[14]

Some proponents of alternative education suggest that each school within a district or geographic area develop its own "alternative" plan. Thus, a principal working with his staff and parents might develop a school program which emphasizes student participation in decision making and development of student self-concept. Another school in the district might stress skill development. A third school might emphasize critical thinking abilities.[15] Other proponents suggest that each school offer several alternative programs simultaneously. Thus, parents and students—and teachers as well—could choose between a program of basic skills, self-concept development, or critical thinking. The school-within-a-school movement is an example of this type of program, although presently the alternatives appear to be limited to "open" education and "traditional" education.

Much additional information about alternative forms schooling can take is available. After examining the works of more than eighty theorists, schools, and projects, Joyce and Weil developed four models to explain the best practices extant in curriculum and instruction. These models are: (1) the social interaction models, (2) the information-processing models, (3) the personal models, and (4) the operant conditioning models.[16]

Social interaction models emphasize the relationship of the person to society and to other people and "reflect a view of human nature which gives priority to social relations and the creation of a better society."[17] Social interaction theorists are represented by Dewey, Thelen, Massialas and Cox, Oliver and Shaver, and the National Training Laboratory (NTL).[18] *Information-processing models* emphasize the development of students to be processors of information. "By information processing we mean the ways in which people handle stimuli from the environment, organize data, sense problems, generate concepts and solutions to problems, and employ verbal and nonverbal symbols."[19] The works of Taba, Suchman, Schwab, Bruner, and Piaget are placed in this model.[20]

Joyce and Weil suggest that the *personal models* share an orientation toward the individual as the source of educational ideas:

> Their frames of reference spotlight personal development and they emphasize the processes by which the individual constructs and organizes his reality. Frequently they emphasize the personal psychology and the emotional life of the individual. . . . Some are concerned with his personality and with his capacity to reach out fearlessly into his milieu to make contact with others. . . . Others are more oriented toward the individual's feeling about himself, toward his self-concept, or his self-image. Yet others are concerned wih helping him develop an authentic reality-oriented view of himself and his society.[21]

The works of Rogers, Glasser, Schutz, Gordon, and Brown are representative of the personal models.[22]

Finally, the fourth set of models described by Joyce and Weil are those referred to as *operant conditioning models.* These have "developed from attempts to create efficient systems for sequencing learning activities and shaping behavior by manipulating reinforcement."[23] They are often referred to as behavior modification because they concentrate upon changing the visible behavior of students rather than underlying or unobservable motivation. Programmed instruction is an obvious example of this model, as is computer-assisted instruction. The works of Skinner, Glaser, and Sullivan fall into this category.[24]

Joyce and Weil suggest that none of these models is discrete: they overlap in purpose and methodology. The critical notion is that alternatives do exist, and they have been and can be operationalized within a school.

We have mixed feelings about the alternative education movement. On the one hand, we believe, as do the advocates of alternative schooling, that the monolithic, bureaucratic tendencies of public schooling must be countered. Further, we believe in pluralistic approaches to schooling with those approaches being determined at the local school level. Finally, we support the notion that schooling can and should be more humane and more "fun" for all involved.

On the other hand, we are concerned about the singlemindedness with which many advocates seem to be approaching the problem of change in schooling. Over the past several decades too many panaceas have been put forth, tried, and come up short of being total solutions for the problems of schooling. Therefore, we must rise above dogmatism and simple solutions and look at the complexities of schooling in a realistic fashion, borrowing from all the knowledge currently available to us as we attempt to improve our schools.

POLITICAL STRATEGIES

Prior to the mid-sixties, educators, by and large, believed that education was apolitical. That is, they thought that schools were somehow above politics and that what happened in schools had little, if anything, to do with the political processes of the surrounding culture. By the end of the sixties, however, it had become obvious to nearly everyone, particularly those attempting to bring about change, that our schools are part of the greater political system and, thus, subject to the political processes of that system. These processes were discussed in Chapter 4.

In the United States, universal public education has traditionally been viewed as a vehicle for providing equality of opportunity to all, and in the past the overwhelming majority of Americans seemed to be prepared to leave the schools alone to get on with the job. A break in this united front came in the 1950s when a vocal right-wing minority began attacking the schools as subversive and "dupes of a communist conspiracy."[25] A "liberal" coalition consisting of minority groups, the poor, intellectuals, and the middle class formed to counter the threat. In the 1960s, however, this coalition began to tear apart. Members of poor and minority communities realized that compensatory programs had either failed or made little progress toward promoting equality. The middle class saw integration and proposed methods of achieving it, such as bussing, as threatening their hard-earned way of life. Both groups turned to political power to express their disenchantment, and both groups made their new power felt. Thus, our frustration with our institutions, our deepening value differences, and our apparent lack of ability to use "normal" procedures to achieve our societal goals have led us as a people to employ newer political strategies for educational change.

As pointed out in earlier chapters, public education has always been "political" in the sense that political processes are utilized to formulate public policy. School boards and state and county school administrations are often elected subunits of city or county government. As with all political systems, demands and supports from the citizenry are formulated, aggregated, and articulated through individuals, special interest groups, and news and other media to those governmental subunits responsible for the formulation of educational policy. These are political processes and there is an ever-growing body of research which is investigating them as such.[26] At the heart of the political process, political scientists tell us, are three key concepts: conflict, power, and policy formation. While these concepts are interrelated, an examination of each can be helpful in placing emerging political change strategies into some kind of educational perspective.

Conflict

Conflict serves as the basis for at least two emerging educational change strategies. On the one hand are those who, largely because of their frustrations with the "system," call for violent acts which they assume will result in change. Strikes, school burnings, marches, sit-ins, and riots are all seen as ways of forcing those in authority to make desired changes. While such means are destructive and often create dangerous counterreactive attitudes against needed change, it must be admitted that much educational change has occurred as a result of such acts during the past decade.

A second educational change strategy, which has a substantial research base, sees conflict as both inevitable and desirable. Most educators are not at all attuned to such a point of view. Typically, school people tend to suppress or avoid conflict assuming that it will go away, though often such suppression leads to even more destructive confrontations at a later date. Those who see conflict as inevitable and desirable suggest that there is a need for "task groups" or cadres of conflict managers who can move into educational settings as objective third parties to assist those who are in conflict to come to some type of compromise on implementing needed changes. This is, of course, very similar to negotiation and arbitration models used by management and labor.[27]

Power

"Power" has become both a political catchword and a political reality in American education. Student power, community power, and teacher power all have made their appearance. Sand recently assessed the implications of the student power movement:

> College students were the first dissenters, but dissension quickly spread to lower levels of education. A survey made recently by the National Association of Secondary School Principals revealed that 59 per cent of the respondents had already experienced some form of student protest, and 56 per cent of the junior highs polled had seen students on the march. Dissatisfaction with the school program, including teachers, curriculum, scheduling, homework, grading, and testing, accounted for student unrest in 45 per cent of the schools responding. Students seemed to be asking for learning based on their own living—for a curriculum that confronted the facts of war, racism, riots, and urban decay and helped them to find remedies for these societal ills as well as answers to the urgent perennial questions, Who am I? Where am I going?
>
> Black students took the protest route, to demonstrate that they no longer intended to remain without pride and ignorant of their own identity and culture. The justice of their complaints hit home in many schools during the sixties. Courses in soul music and Swahili, black history, and black culture began to multiply. Textbook publishers rushed to the presses with new books designed to make amends for years of neglect of

the contributions of black people to American history. It is obvious that student power cannot be ignored, laughed out of existence, or swept under the rug. In many instances, student power has been a restraining force to change when it led to violence. However, student power, along with community and teacher power, is potentially among the strongest supporting forces for really making change happen.[28]

Speaking of community power, Sand continued:

Parent power has been burgeoning, too, in the late sixties, and from an unexpected quarter—the ghetto. Poverty area and minority group parents were hotly protesting the dismal statistical truth that the longer their children stayed in school, the further behind they fell. These parents began seeking the same control over their children's education that they believed suburban parents exercised. Decentralization and community control became their rallying cries.

Urban parents demanded—and in some instances got—control of their schools. In some cases, community control became a bitterly contested end in itself. But in others it was a step toward a cooperative restructuring that involved all segments of the school community. Experiments in widespread community participation in schools have not always been successful, as we have seen in Brooklyn's Ocean Hill Brownsville District. The Morgan Community School and the Anacostia Community Demonstration District, both in Washington, D.C., have, on the other hand, been able to make headway in involving the community in the schools. Each has a community board to determine school policy. Boston and Chicago have also begun to experiment with citizen participation and the utilization of external resources.[29]

Teachers, too, have power, and they, too, have begun to use it. Such power, expressed mainly in strikes and other union activities, has been used, by and large, for obtaining needed higher salaries and benefits. Unfortunately, teacher power has yet to focus on the vital issue that would win them widespread public support—improvement of instruction. For example, the central thrust of the major professional associations, the American Federation of Teachers (AFT) and the National Education Association (NEA), has been to assure that there continues to be one credentialed teacher for each twenty-five children in a self-contained classroom in each school in America. Their focus has been on the salary that teacher is to receive. Such organizations would do well to use their newfound power to support not only their own welfare but also instructional improvement and the monitoring of their own ranks with the goals of (1) raising standards, (2) building some type of internship system like that of the medical profession,

(3) retraining themselves, and (4) removing incompetency from their ranks. It should also be pointed out that using teacher power to gain economic benefits in a time of economic limitations could ultimately do damage both to education and to the goals of organized teachers themselves.

Fantini summarizes the potential for the various power movements as follows:

> The participants who lead reform in the 70's will be those closest to the action—teachers, parents and students. Participation of these three publics in the governance of urban schools carries the potential for triggering change in substance and personnel. If all that were to happen under the new participatory movement would be a shift in control, so that a new group controlled the schools as an end in itself, the educational institution would remain outdated. The hope, however, is that those seeking control will use their political energy to set in motion the search for institutional renewal at the local school level where it counts.[30]

Policy Formation

Power in school systems, as in all political systems, results from control of public policy and control of vital resources such as jobs, funds, social status, and expertise. Competition among groups for the right to make policy and for the resources of power generally makes for a dynamic, pluralistic, and changing system, whereas bureaucratic monopolies generally produce a static system. Historically, administrators have used their expertise and position to secure greater control over jobs and funds. In so doing, they have expanded their control over public education policy so that others have largely been excluded from policy making.[31]

With the advent of the various power movements discussed above, some promising new configurations of policy formation have begun to emerge on the American educational scene. These are new federal-state-local relationships, metropolitan planning, and decentralization.

The federal enabling legislation of the sixties upset the balance of power in American education and, in fact, encouraged community power since much federal money went directly to local communities, bypassing the states. New relationships were formed and significant changes were brought about in the realm of policy formation. Similarly now, state-local relationships are shifting somewhat in part due to revenue sharing and the subsequent growth in importance of state departments of education. What is happening is that state departments through their categorical programs (e.g., bilingual education, early childhood education, compensatory education) are dealing directly with schools regarding such matters as guidelines and evaluation. In so doing, they are in many ways bypassing the school districts with whom they formerly worked more closely. Such a shift is reinforced by the decentralization movement and by statewide testing programs. As discussed in Chapter 4, there are those who fear that the ultimate result could be a loss of local control and the emergence of statewide systems of education.

As one means of distributing power, Nystrand and Cunningham have proposed what they call "Federated Urban School Systems."[32] Such "metropolitan" systems, organized across urban-suburban lines, would at once deal with two vital problems which now plague American education and American society—integration and the equalization of fiscal resources.[33] The common assumption is that only the cities will benefit, though there is evidence that suburbs will profit from metropolitan fiscal arrangements in some standard metropolitan areas because property taxes raised from the highly industrialized cities could be distributed, in part, to the suburbs.[34]

There are serious obstacles to the implementation of such a model in metropolitan areas. First, we pointed out earlier the problem of polarization among various groups in our society. People seek housing, work, and social and educative settings in which others like themselves are in the majority. Second, metropolitan cooperation would require some redistribution of property tax monies. Finally, consolidation of multiple school districts presents legal problems and problems of vested interest on the part of school administrators who would view themselves as losing power. Even so, it is probable that metropolitan cooperation will grow as a means of solving our great social and economic problems, including the problem of improving our schools.

Community control and decentralization are movements which arise from our inherent national distrust of bigness, be it bigness in business or government. More importantly, these concepts arise from our knowledge that bureaucratic school systems have been less than responsive to particular local needs. Major cities, such as New York, Cleveland, Boston, Los Angeles, Newark, Detroit, Washington, D.C., Philadelphia, and Chicago, have all implemented decentralization plans. Others are following or will follow suit.

For many, decentralization implies moving decision making and related accountability to local schools so that they can serve the needs of their communities by finding a variety of means and paths for reaching the common goals of education. Watson states this position when he says:

> The key element in rebuilding urban school systems to facilitate improved educational opportunities may be decentralization. Frequently confused with community control, decentralization actually implies a shift from generalized impersonal decision making to allowing decisions to be made as close as possible to the action, the interface between teacher and child. Although broad policies may still be set by a central board, implementation will be planned and carried out locally, with due regard for local needs, interests and resources.[35]

The move to decentralize decision making in American education holds much promise. It also has major problems. Most important, it runs the risk of creating false expectations in and struggles for power among administrators, teachers, parents, and community groups with vested interests. The critical problem found in current efforts to decentralize is that while the intention is to get decision making to levels as close as possible to the learner, just who should make what decisions is not clear, as pointed out in Chapter 4. The clarification of decision-making roles and responsibilities and training for such roles should be prerequisites to decentralization in order to avoid false expectations and power vacuums.

Education has become politicized, and there are several political change strategies which hold promise, especially the "grass roots" involvement implied in decentralization. If our institutions are to remain vital and self-renewing, people will need to be involved and active. Such involvement can well lead to the establishment of alternative or pluralistic models of schooling, which would have the effect of making our educational system more relevant and of strengthening our society.

Finally, if we move to shift our basic policy-making strategies through metropolitan arrangements and through strengthened federal-state-local relationships, eventually we may be able to solve many of our social problems, including the provision of quality education and equality of educational opportunity for all.

PEER SUPPORT STRATEGIES

We began in Chapter 1 by stressing the importance of the single school as the significant unit for educational change. Our bias is easily understood when it is noted that for five years we were associated with a project which attempted to experiment with and document the potential strengths and weaknesses of a change strategy which focused upon the single school. That strategy was developed in the League of Cooperating Schools which was made up of eighteen collaborating schools and school districts in southern California.[36]

The primary notion behind this strategy is that if meaningful change is to occur, schools must be self-renewing and able to solve their problems as they arise.[37] Four of the major assumptions which serve as the foundation for this strategy are set forth by Bentzen and Tye, as follows:

> (a) The single school is the appropriate target unit for an intervention designed to develop self-renewal capabilities; (b) any group of single schools contains a large pool of resources which can be mobilized for group self-help; (c) the key to a self-renewing school lies in its staff's focus on decision-making processes; and (d) the most effective and most economical mechanism for developing and supporting self-renewing schools is a peer group system of single schools.[38]

If a school is to be self-renewing, it must be able to control and utilize whatever outside professional resources are available to it. Typically, school systems are not structured so that this can occur, and usually consultant help is allocated by the school district. Even where a special project or program (e.g., Title I–ESEA) is in operation, the school has no guarantee that it can determine its own consultant needs. And when a special project ends, consultants are no longer available to the school.

Even if a school could control its own consultant resources, there would be a serious problem. Teachers and principals tend to have an ambivalent attitude toward outside experts. On the one hand, they expect them to provide all the answers. On the other, the staff often feels that the expert is not really aware of all the day-to-day problems of keeping school. In addition, the expert-client relationship, which is based on the authority-influence strategy discussed in the previous chapter, is not necessarily conducive to developing in the staff the abilities it needs to bring about change in the school.

Experience in the League of Cooperating Schools suggests that much help can come from other teachers within the school and from other schools if some sort of cooperative linkage is established between schools. This sharing of resources has three distinct advantages. First, it is seen by teachers and principals as highly relevant, since help comes from other teachers and principals who are engaged daily in similar activities. Second, the amount and number of potential resources is greatly increased. Third, a school staff becomes both a giver and receiver of help, thus developing the process of self-renewal from two directions.

If the single school is to become self-renewing, the staff not only needs resources to help it but must also be able to develop a process for solving collective problems. The problem-solving process was discussed at length in Chapter 6. It only remains to conclude:

> The quality of the . . . process in any school can be judged by several criteria, but its most salient characteristic in most schools is its relatively low visibility to the staff. Therefore, the first step toward building self-renewing schools is to create in the staff a constant awareness of the way in which things do or do not get done. With that awareness, each staff can seek the resources it needs to adjust its [problem-solving] process to meet its goals and can socialize new members at a high level of introspection about [problem solving].[39]

In the League of Cooperating Schools, the intervention strategy which emerged involved building a peer group of schools which shared each other's resources and problems and which expected one another to focus upon a problem-solving process. Thus, at once, a new set of norms (problem solving) and a new set of supports (shared resources) were built in as a means of developing self-renewing behavior and of minimizing dependence upon outside experts.

The role of the interventionist became that of a facilitator of interaction among school staffs. This can be a problem, for the typical interventionist does not attempt to cause schools to look to themselves for answers. Typically, his satisfactions come from playing the role of "expert." Bentzen articulates this view as follows:

> We are apparently victims of years of schooling which have continually reinforced the notion that if we ask around long enough, we will find someone with superior knowledge who can, with relative ease, offer solutions to our problems. So, we see school staffs waiting to be told what to do. . . . So, too, we see the experts eager to tell the schools what to do. Most of those who play the interventionist role have a true commitment to helping schools improve and an honest belief that they can be of most help by imparting to school staffs, in one way or another, some kind of "higher-level" information. . . .
>
> Indeed, school staffs need to gain perspective on their problems, do need to learn a variety of new skills, but our observations have been that

the breakthrough insights that result in truly changed behavior in principals and teachers usually come from sharing information with others who they know face the same daily situation that they do. It is unfortunate that many who play the role of expert-interventionist perceive such exchanges as mere exercises in "pooling ignorance"—as if their own usefulness depended upon the existence of ignorance in others.[40]

|I|D|E|A|, in creating the League of Cooperating Schools, attempted to overcome traditional forces of resistance to change by creating a countervailing force consisting of many schools in a variety of school districts drawn together in a new social system. However, as Culver and her associates point out, it is not impossible to create such a social system within the single school or within a single school district.[41] Drawing upon the League experience, these writers suggest such strategies as having teachers observe each other and discuss their observations, establishing representative decision-making committees and task forces in the school and district, holding "open houses" for teachers from nearby schools, organizing workshops in which teachers teach each other, publishing and circulating a newsletter written by teachers in which they discuss their ideas, utilizing teachers as experts and as consultants to each other, and sharing consultants among teachers with common needs from two or more schools.

The peer group problem-solving strategy holds much promise for bringing about schools that will have more control over shaping their own destinies. In short, it is a strategy which holds the potential for building self-renewing schools.[42]

CONCLUSION

Upgrading of personnel, better management, alternative education, politics, and building self-renewing schools are all emerging on the educational scene as means of creating better schools. As dissimilar as these strategies may seem, they have at least one thing in common. They are formative. That is, they are in the process of becoming. It is through these strategies that we will begin to shape the schools of tomorrow, and we invite those in the school to join in this task.

NOTES

1 See, for example, the Temple City, California, Plan described in M. John Rand and Fenwick English, "Towards a Differentiated Teaching Staff," *Phi Delta Kappan*, vol. 49, pp. 264–268, January 1968.

2 The Ocean View School District in Huntington Beach, California, has evolved a plan whereby when a teaching vacancy occurs in a given school, that staff receives x amount of dollars. The staff then decides whether they need a new classroom teacher, specialist, aides, part-time personnel, or the like. For information, contact Dale Coogan, District Superintendent, Oceanview School District, 7972 Warner Avenue, Huntington Beach, California 92647.

3 *Education Summary,* National School Public Relations Association, Washington, D.C., Nov. 6, 1972.

4 See, Raymond E. Callahan, *Education and the Cult of Efficiency,* The University of Chicago Press, Chicago, 1962.

5 Ewald Nyquist, quoted in *Accountability: Review of Literature and Recommendations for Implementation,* North Carolina Department of Public Instruction, Divisions of Planning, Research, and Development, May 1972, p. 3.

6 Terry D. Cornell, *Performances and Process Objectives,* Educational Innovators Press, Tucson, Ariz., 1970, p. 6.

7 David Selden, "Productivity, Yes. Accountability, No," *Nation's Schools,* vol. 89, pp. 5ff., May 1972.

8 Mary M. Bentzen and Kenneth A. Tye, "Effecting Change in Elementary Schools," in John I. Goodlad and Harold G. Shane (eds.), *The Elementary School in the United States,* Seventy-second Yearbook of the National Society for the Study of Education, Part II, The University of Chicago Press, Chicago, 1973, p. 366.

9 Leon M. Lessinger, *Every Kid a Winner: Accountability in Education,* Simon and Schuster, New York, 1970.

10 "Performance Contracting," |I|D|E|A| *Reporter,* Institute for Development of Educational Activities, Inc., Information and Services Division, Melbourne, Fla., Winter 1970.

11 See, for example: John Holt, *How Children Learn,* Pitman, New York, 1967; George B. Leonard, *Education and Ecstasy,* Delacorte Press, New York, 1968; William Glasser, *Schools Without Failure,* Harper & Row, New York, 1969; Herbert R. Kohl, *The Open Classroom: A Practical Guide to a New Way of Teaching,* Random House, Vintage Books, New York, 1969; Carl R. Rogers, *Freedom to Learn,* Merrill, Columbus, Ohio, 1969; Ivan D. Illich, *The Celebration of Awareness: A Call for Institutional Revolution,* Doubleday, Garden City, N.Y., 1970.

12 Vernon H. Smith, "Options in Public Education: The Quiet Revolution," *Phi Delta Kappan,* vol. 54, pp. 434–435, March 1973.

13 Mario Fantini, "Alternatives within Public Schools," *Phi Delta Kappan,* vol. 54, pp. 444–448, March 1973.

14 Ibid., p. 445.

15 Such a plan is set forth in Richard C. Williams, "A Plan for an Accountable Elementary School District," in Carmen M. Culver and Gary J. Hoban (eds.), *The Power to Change: Issues for the Innovative Educator,* McGraw-Hill, New York, 1973, pp. 221–244.

16 Bruce Joyce and Marsha Weil, *Models of Teaching,* Prentice-Hall, Englewood Cliffs, N.J., 1972.

17 Ibid., p. 9.

18 See, for example, John Dewey, *Democracy and Education,* Macmillan, New York, 1916; Herbert Thelen, *Education and the Human Quest,* Harper & Row, New York, 1960; Byron Massialas and Benjamin Cox, *Inquiry in Social Studies,* McGraw-Hill, New York, 1966; Donald W. Oliver and James P. Shaver, *Teaching Public Issues in the High School,* Houghton-Mifflin, Boston, 1966; Leland P. Bradford, "Developing Potentials through Class Groups," in Leland P. Bradford (ed.), *Human Forces in Teaching and Learning,* National Education Association, National Training Laboratory, Washington, D.C., 1961.

19 Joyce and Weil, op. cit., p. 9.

20 See, for example: Hilda Taba, *Teacher's Handbook for Elementary Social Studies,* Addison-Wesley, Reading, Mass., 1967; J. Richard Suchman, *Inquiry Development Program: Developing Inquiry,* Science Research Associates, 1966; Joseph J. Schwab, Supervisor, Biological Sciences Curriculum Study, *Biology Teachers Handbook,* Wiley, New York, 1965; Jerome Bruner, Jacqueline J. Goodnow, and George A. Austin, *A Study of Thinking,* Science Editions, Inc., New York, 1967; Hans G. Furth, *Piaget and Knowledge,* Prentice-Hall, Englewood Cliffs, N.J., 1969.

21 Joyce and Weil, op. cit., p. 10.

22 See, for example: Rogers, op. cit.; Glasser, op. cit.; William Schutz, *Joy: Expanding Human Awareness,* Grove Press, New York, 1967; William J. Gordon, *The Metaphorical Way of Learning and Knowing,* Synectics Education Press, Cambridge, Mass., 1970; George Brown, *Human Teaching for Human Learning,* Viking, New York, 1971.

23 Joyce and Weil, op. cit., p. 10.

24 See, for example: B. F. Skinner, *Beyond Freedom and Dignity,* Knopf, New York, 1971; Julian Taber, Robert Glaser, and H. Schaeffer Halmuth, *Learning and Programmed Instruction,* Addison-Wesley, Reading, Mass., 1965; M. W. Sullivan, *Programmed English: A Modern Grammar for High School and College Students,* Macmillan, New York, 1963.

25 See Willis W. Harman, *The Nature of Our Changing Society: Impli-
    cations for Schools,* ERIC Clearinghouse on Educational Administra-
    tion, Eugene, Oreg., 1969; and Mary Anne Raywid, *The Ax-Grinders,*
    Macmillan, New York, 1962.

26 Political systems and analysis emerged as a field of study during the
    mid-sixties. See for example: David Easton, *A Framework for Politi-
    cal Analysis,* Prentice-Hall, Englewood Cliffs, N.J., 1965; Gabriel A.
    Almond and G. Bingham Powell, Jr., *Comparative Politics: A Devel-
    opmental Approach,* Little, Brown, Boston, Mass., 1966; William
    C. Mitchell, *Sociological Analysis and Politics: The Theories of
    Talcott Parsons,* Prentice-Hall, Englewood Cliffs, 1967. At the Uni-
    versity of California, Los Angeles, a series of doctoral dissertations
    has utilized political systems analysis in the study of the politics of
    education under the leadership of Professor Jay D. Scribner. Some of
    these are Wallace I. Homitz, "A Study of Demand upon the School
    Boards in a Unified and an Independent Junior College District,"
    1967; Walter Pentz, "The Effect of Population Changes upon the
    Demands Made by the Public and Junior College Trustees," 1967;
    Kenneth A. Tye, "A Conceptual System for Political Analysis: Public
    Demands and School Board Decisions," 1968; Owen Knox, "Process-
    ing Environmental Demands: A Case Study for Decentralization,"
    1971; Bruce C. Newlin, "Proportional Representation and the Win-
    ton Act: A Functional-Systems Analysis," 1971; Emory H. Holmes,
    "Community Representation in Educational Decision Making: An
    Exploratory Case Study of School-Community Advisory Councils,"
    1972.

27 Kenneth A. Tye, "The Political Linkage Agent," in Ronald G. Have-
    lock and Mary Havelock, *Training for Change Agents,* Center for
    Research Utilization of Scientific Knowledge (CRUSK), Institute for
    Social Research, Ann Arbor, Mich., 1972. See also Mark Chesler et
    al., "Affecting Political and Structural Change in Schools," in ibid.

28 Ole Sand, "Strategies for Change," in *The Curriculum: Retrospect
    And Prospect,* National Society for the Study of Education, Seven-
    tieth Yearbook, Part I, The University of Chicago Press, Chicago,
    1971, p. 221.

29 Ibid., p. 222.

30 Quoted in Ibid., p. 223.

31 For a more detailed discussion, see Marilyn Gittell, "The Balance of
    Power and the Community School," in Henry M. Levin (ed.), *Com-
    munity Control of Schools,* Brookings, Washington, D.C., 1970;
    Marilyn Gittell and T. Edward Hollander, *Six Urban School Districts:
    A Comparative Study of Institutional Response,* Praeger, New York,

1968; Peter Schrag, "Boston: Education's Last Hurrah," *Saturday Review*, May 21, 1966, pp. 56–58.

32   Raphael O. Nystrand and Luvern L. Cunningham, "Federated Urban School Systems: Compromising the Centralization-Decentralization Issue," in Frank W. Lutz (ed.), *Toward Improved Urban Education*, Charles A. Jones, Worthington, Ohio, 1970, pp. 95–111.

33   Robert J. Havighurst (ed.), *Metropolitanism: Its Challenges to Education*, National Society for the Study of Education, Sixty-seventh Yearbook, Part I, The University of Chicago Press, Chicago, 1968.

34   Advisory Committee on Intergovernmental Relations, *Metropolitan Social and Economic Disparities: Implications for Intergovernmental Relations in Central Cities and Suburbs*, U.S. Government Printing Office, Washington, D.C., 1965.

35   Bernard C. Watson, "Rebuilding the System: Practical Goal or Impossible Dream?" *Phi Delta Kappan*, vol. 52, p. 352, February 1971.

36   The project, entitled "The Study of Educational Change and School Improvement," was conducted by the Research Division of the Institute for Development of Educational Activities (|I|D|E|A|), Los Angeles, 1966–1971. The full report of the strategy and results is reported in Mary M. Bentzen, *Changing Schools: The Magic Feather Principle*, McGraw-Hill, New York, 1974, a companion volume to this book in the Series on Educational Change of the |I|D|E|A| Reports on Schooling. Districts involved were Fountain Valley School District, Timber School District, Los Angeles Unified School District, San Diego City Schools, Santa Monica Unified School District, Culver City Unified School District, Alvord Unified School District, Corona-Norco School District, Pasadena City Schools, Lompoc Unified School District, Santa Barbara City Schools, Inglewood Unified School District, Bellflower Unified School District, Central School District, Delano Union School District, Poway Unified School District, Riverside Unified School District, Simi Valley Unified School District.

37   The notion of self-renewing institutions is discussed in John Gardner, *Self-Renewal: The Individual and the Innovative Society*, Harper & Row, New York, 1963. The school as a self-renewing institution is discussed in Matthew B. Miles and Dale Lake, "Self-Renewal in School Systems: A Strategy for Planned Change," in Goodwin Watson (ed.), *Concepts for Social Change*, National Training Laboratory, Institute for Applied Behavioral Science, Washington, D.C., 1967.

38   Bentzen and Tye, op. cit., p. 371.

39   Ibid., p. 374.

40   Mary M. Bentzen, "A Peer Group Strategy for Intervention in

Schools," unpublished paper, Institute for Development of Educational Activities, Inc., Research Division, Los Angeles, 1970.

41   Carmen M. Culver, David A. Shiman, and Ann Lieberman, "Working Together: The Peer Group Strategy," in Culver and Hoban (eds.), op. cit., p. 94.

42   For a definition and discussion of the self-renewing school see Bentzen, *Changing Schools,* pp. 61–74.

CHAPTER 8
TOWARD SELF-RENEWING SCHOOLS

The underlying assumption of this book has been that schools are going to change. We also assume that practitioners in the school can play an active leadership role in bringing about such change. Finally, we assume that the school as a unit, not the classroom nor the district, is where change efforts should be concentrated if an optimum environment for learning and living is to be created.

The intent of this book is to draw together materials from existing literature on educational change in order to assist practitioners in defining their role as change agents, to assist them in viewing the school as a unit undergoing change, and to provide them with an enlightened perspective as they consider making changes. Having acquired knowledge of the future and what it means for schools, an understanding of the school as a social system residing in a sociopolitical context, insight into the change process itself, and a repertoire of alternative change strategies, practitioners are in a position to bring about meaningful and thoughtful improvement in schooling.

What follows is an attempt to formulate a series of practically oriented recommendations. It is our view that if such recommendations are accepted and implemented, practitioners will be able to build self-renewing schools wherein improvement will become a continuous process. First, we will address recommendations to those outside of the school who set policy or administer school systems. It is these people who make it possible (or impossible) for the people in the school to meet their goals. We then address ourselves to the people in the school—teachers and principals.

RECOMMENDATIONS TO SCHOOL-DISTRICT OFFICIALS

Obviously, school-district administrators and local boards of education are constrained in what they can do by state and federal laws, regulations, and policies. They are further constrained by the actions of state and federal officials and by the attitudes and wants of the members of the community. Most of all, they are constrained by a cultural reality which presently involves great uncertainty about the values we hold as a nation, about the purposes we hold for schooling, and about who shall make what educational decisions. These constraints, however, need not stop those at the district level from moving ahead to facilitate the development of self-renewing schools.

Our work in the "vineyards" of school change, together with our review of pertinent literature and research, lead us to make the following recommendations to school-district officials dedicated to the development of self-renewing schools.

Recommendation 1   District administrators and school board members must involve themselves, community representatives, and representatives from the schools in continuous and serious dialogue about the purposes of schooling as these purposes relate to the district and the children they serve (see Chapters 1 and 4).

> Such discussions must be data based. That is, they should be conducted with a knowledge of such things as current community needs and wants, student needs and wants, demographic characteristics of the community, and predicted trends in society as a whole.
>
> Such discussions must be continuous and not take the form of "one time" needs assessment or goal-setting activities.
>
> Such discussions must be open, allowing for a wide range of opinions to be expressed. Information about these discussions and their conclusions should be reported widely in the community and in the schools.
>
> Statements of purpose resulting from these discussions should serve as a major basis for policy formulation by the board of education and as a foundation for administrative action on the part of district administrators.
>
> Periodic assessments of schooling in the district should be carried out and judged against the articulated purposes of schooling.

Recommendation 2   School districts must begin to build support systems which assist schools to become self-renewing institutions.

> The district should take the position that the school is the critical unit for

change and behave as if it believed such a statement to be true. Working toward a "Y-minded" philosophy based upon trust would be a good first step (see Chapter 6).

Districts should train or employ personnel given the responsibility of assisting schools to develop skills in communication, group dynamics, conflict solution, value clarification, decision-making and problem-solving processes. These "change agents" do not necessarily need to be added on to the system. Many people presently serving as supervisors or coordinators could perform such roles (see Chapters 3, 5, and 6).

Districts should reach outward to link with agencies having potential as resources to schools. These include (1) research and development centers and universities willing to conduct research on, or assist in, the development of school-based projects, (2) teacher-training institutions willing to design pre-service and in-service training programs based upon school needs, (3) information centers such as ERIC, and (4) community agencies and individuals willing to assist with school programs (see Chapters 1, 2, 4, and 6).

Districts should build and maintain internal linkages and communications among schools—leagues of cooperating schools—with common purposes, problems, and programs and with the intention of sharing resources, ideas, and norms for improvement (see Chapter 7).

The service function of all personnel employed as "staff" at the district level should be clearly communicated with emphasis upon the fact that they do not hold line authority (see Chapters 3 and 4).

As schools become more self-directing, the district should provide them with consultation in those areas where they have not had experience, such as setting criteria and establishing procedures for selection and purchase of materials, preparing funding proposals, and conducting research. However, the district should not make decisions about such matters for schools (see Chapter 6).

Schools need time to grow and become self-renewing. Districts should place a very high priority on affording time for schools to plan with latitude to enable them to decide how such time should be spent (see Chapter 7).

Recommendation 3   School districts should begin to eliminate barriers which stand in the way of schools becoming self-renewing institutions.

"Know thyself" is still a sound and appropriate adage. School-district officials should conduct an in-depth analysis of structure, procedures and behaviors in an effort to identify authoritarian or paternalistic practices which inhibit the development of self-renewing schools (see Chapters 4, 5, and 6).

Board members and school-district officials themselves should undergo training in communication, group dynamics, conflict resolution, value clarification, decision-making and problem-solving skills and processes (see Chapters 1, 4, 5, and 6).

Points of decision making within the district should be clearly articulated to all groups involved in the day-to-day operation of the school district (board members, line administrators, professional support personnel, classified personnel, community representatives, parents, students, and teachers). Clarification is essential to any effort to decentralize decision making to the local school (see Chapters 5 and 7).

Institutional change must be viewed as a systemic phenomenon. Districts must recognize that any single change in a school will create other changes. Such contingencies should be planned for (see Chapters 3, 4, 5, and 7).

Guidelines for federal and state categorical programs cause school staffs to spend countless hours on paperwork and other bureaucratic activities. Meeting such guidelines frequently has dramatic and negative effects upon structures, roles, norms, and processes in the local school. School-district officials should attempt to use whatever means they have to simplify such guidelines (for example, through professional associations or through personal contact with legislators or state officials). While national and state priorities represented by categorical programs are important, districts must consider not accepting monies if, in fact, the receipt of such monies adds to the bureaucratization of the district or impedes the development of self-renewing schools (see Chapter 4).

The accountability movement, despite rhetoric to the contrary, is both bureaucratic and authoritarian in its thrust. To be sure, people in schools need to be responsible for their actions, but we recommend that such responsibility be built not through "scientifically" managing people but rather moving toward a climate wherein people can grow and demonstrate their responsibility (see Chapters 4 and 7).

Recommendation 4   District personnel should recognize that American education is political in nature and begin to take a proactive rather than reactive stance toward political issues which affect the ability of schools to become self-renewing.

Districts must recognize "community power" as a reality. Districts need to determine (1) what areas of decision making are in fact appropriate at the community level, (2) what structures hold the best promise for bringing about community involvement, and (3) what procedures can be employed to guarantee open and honest interaction between the community and the system (see Chapters 1, 4, and 7).

"Teacher power" must be accepted. Organized teachers are reacting largely to authoritarianism and frustration created by bureaucratic structures. Remove these and one conflict dimension is eliminated. Teachers are concerned about students. Build self-renewing structures within which they see themselves as improving the student's lot and another conflict dimension is removed. Organized teachers often act out of self-interest (salaries and benefits). These should be recognized as legitimate and negotiated realistically at the district level (see Chapters 3, 4, and 7).

"Government power" must be dealt with. Federal and state politicians are earnestly searching for solutions to the problems which beset our nation. While they often appear to be making unreasonable or even harmful demands upon schools, the fact is that most of them have deep commitment to public education. School-district officials through personal contacts and through professional organizations must seek to establish new and cooperative interaction with legislators and other government officials so that the need to develop self-renewing schools is clearly understood and ultimately facilitated (see Chapters 1, 3, 4, 5, and 6).

Districts must realize that other school districts face similar problems. District administrators should seek consciously to share problems, needs, information, solutions, and resources with each other across district boundaries. The notion of federated school districts should be explored (see Chapter 7).

No recommendations which have been stated so far, nor any which will follow, require additional monies to implement. If we need to buy time for people to think, interact and plan, this can be built into all proposals for funding or into existing budgets. The problem is one of priorities. One needs to ask the question, "Why do we do what we are doing and are there better ways?" (see Chapters 1, 4, and 5).

Recommendation 5   School-district officials should seriously reexamine their personnel policies. People are the key ingredient in the educational endeavor.

School-district officials, involving representatives of concerned groups, should consider the development of early retirement programs for school personnel, which are not arbitrary and give people options on how they wish to spend their later productive years (see Chapter 7).

School-district officials, along with representatives of concerned groups, should help schools establish thoughtful criteria for the selection of school personnel. These criteria should move beyond the technical-skill level to include such things as openness, willingness to learn, emphathy, internal locus of control, concern for others, creativity, motivation, and social awareness. This is particularly critical for people who will be in positions of leadership. Further, school districts should make such criteria known to training institutions (see Chapter 7).

Recommendation 6 School-district officials should encourage, support, and assist schools in their efforts to build alternative programs for the populations they serve in the belief that our pluralistic society must be preserved (see Chapter 7).

Recommendation 7 School-district officials should help school personnel develop programs which are directed at meeting the needs of individual students who will live in the future. Such a move serves to implement statements of educational purpose calling for schools to be designed as places where people can reach self-fulfillment and where they can prepare for the future (see Chapter 2).

Recommendation 8 School-district officials should assist school personnel in better assessing what they do, how they do it and what they can do more efficiently. We do not know enough about how our schools operate. Achievement-test scores are not an adequate basis for deciding what changes should be brought about and how (see Chapters 1, 2, 3, 5, 6, and 7).

RECOMMENDATIONS FOR PEOPLE IN THE SCHOOL

People who work in schools every day—principals, teachers, and others —often feel impotent. So many decisions have been made for them for so long that they have become dependent. Those school practitioners who have tried to create changes—and who have become frustrated in the process—tend to do one of several things: (1) give up and accede to the "system," staying in their jobs and usually resisting exhortations to change, (2) leave the profession, (3) join "power" groups which seem to hold some promise for creating change, or (4) search out other educational positions which allow them to be more creative.

But there are other options. We feel strongly that there are ways in which practitioners can make their schools not only better places to work but also better places for children to learn. A first step might be for district officials to implement the recommendations set forth above. But even if they do not, there are activities that can be undertaken in the individual school to bring about change. Listed below are a series of recommendations to aid a principal and teachers in working on improving their school.

Recommendation 1   School personnel should involve themselves with community representatives and students in continuous and serious discussions of the purposes of the school (see Chapters 1 and 4).

> Such discussions should be data based. That is, they should be conducted with knowledge of such things as current community needs and wants, student needs and wants, demographic characteristics of the community, and predicted trends in the larger society.
>
> Such discussions should not take the form of "one time" needs assessment or goal-setting activities.
>
> Such discussions should be open, allowing for the expression of varied and diverse opinions. The results of these discussions should be reported widely in the community and in the schools using all available media.
>
> Statements of purpose resulting from such discussions should correlate with those developed at the district level. Where there are differences between school and district purposes—and there might well be—these differences should be clearly documented and understood by all concerned. Purposes determined at the school level should prevail when an adequate process has been employed in their establishment.
>
> All activities within the school (curriculum, organization, employment of personnel, etc.) should be carried out in light of the stated purposes of the school.
>
> Periodic assessments of school accomplishments should be carried out using the stated purposes as criteria. Such assessments should lead to periodic revisions of purposes and programs.

Recommendation 2   Schools should begin to build support systems which allow people to become self-renewing and collaborating individuals.

> A schoolwide support system should be created in the belief that the school is the critical unit for improvement. The adoption of a "Y-minded" philosophy based upon trust would be a good first step (see Chapter 6).
>
> School staffs, along with appropriate community representatives, should involve themselves in in-service activities directed at improving skills in communication, group dynamics, conflict resolution, value clarification, decision-making and problem-solving processes (see Chapters 3, 5, and 6).
>
> Schools should build and maintain outward linkages to agencies which can serve as resources. These include: (1) research and development centers and universities willing to conduct research or assist in the

development of school-based projects, (2) teacher training institutions willing to design pre-service and in-service training programs based upon school needs, (3) information centers such as ERIC, (4) intermediate units and service centers, (5) school-district resources, and (6) community agencies and individuals willing to assist with school programs (see Chapters 1, 2, 4, and 6).

Schools should build linkages between and among themselves. The intent is for people in the schools to share their own resources, ideas, problems, and norms for improvement. In some cases, such linkages will be by level of schooling (for example, elementary schools working together). In other cases, all levels will want to work together. Such arrangements need not be formal. Principals can be the key to bringing about such linkages (see Chapter 7).

In order to plan adequately, school personnel need to have time. It is not unreasonable to think in terms of a four-day instructional week with a fifth day set aside for planning while students are engaged in out-of-school activities. Even without district support for minimum days or paid substitutes, there are many ways those in the school can find additional time for planning. For example, the principal might take over a class, team-teaching arrangements could provide periodic free time, aids or paraprofessionals could work with groups or individual children. The possibilities are endless if teachers and principal work together to explore them (see Chapter 7).

The principal is critical to the change process in the school. His task should be viewed as that of leader, facilitator, and resource person—not that of administrator, manager, and authority (see Chapter 5).

Recommendation 3   Schools should begin to eliminate barriers which stand in the way of their becoming self-renewing institutions.

Isolation of individuals and groups—teachers from each other, teachers from parents and the community, teachers from administrators, administrators from students—is a major deterrent to both individual and institutional renewal. Every effort should be made to overcome such isolation through building group problem-solving and decision-making structures (see Chapters 2, 3, and 7).

"Know thyself" is still as sound at the personal and school level as it is at the district level. The people in the school, working together, should conduct an in-depth analysis of structures, procedures, and behaviors in an effort to determine where authoritarian practices exist, where communication is inadequate, and where decision-making roles are unclear (see Chapters 4, 5, and 6).

Decision-making roles within the school should be clearly defined by those involved in the day-to-day operation of the school (principal, teachers, specialists, aides, students, parents, and community representatives). Such clarification is essential if the school is to integrate its diverse activities and really become a "unit of change" (see Chapters 3, 5, and 7).

A school is a complex social system. Thus, those in the school must recognize that any single change brought about in the school will create other changes (for example, adding coordinating personnel to the staff changes communication, decision-making, and influence processes). Such contingencies should be anticipated and planned for (see Chapters 3, 4, 5, and 7).

If schools enter federal and state categorical programs, they are required to spend a good deal of time in assessing, evaluating, and reporting. All proposals written for such funds should include requests for monies which will cover the personnel and time for these activities. Otherwise, monies received may not be worth the stress they place on the school (see Chapter 4).

The accountability movement is a reality. While present implementation often appears to be or, in fact, is authoritarian in thrust, it can be a positive force encouraging healthy change in schools. Educationists need to be responsible for their actions. Responsibility, however, is best borne by people who have contributed to development of purposes, trust, cooperation, and respect (see Chapters 3, 4, and 7).

Recommendation 4   School personnel should begin to take proactive rather than reactive stances toward political issues which can affect school programs (sex education, methods of teaching reading, and teaching about communism).

"Community involvement" is a reality. School personnel need to work with community representatives to determine (1) what areas of decision making are appropriate for community members to be involved in, (2) what structures hold the best promise for bringing about such involvement, and (3) what procedures should be employed to guarantee open and honest interaction between the community and school. A continual two-way information flow between community and school is essential. Gate-keeping and public-relations approaches to the community will no longer suffice (see Chapters 1, 4, and 7).

There is a real necessity to distinguish between the organized teachers who are demanding a share in policy making at the district level and individual teachers in the school who desire to work together toward

improved instruction for students. The building of self-renewing structures at the school level is neither dependent upon nor in opposition
to the goals of organized teacher groups (see Chapters 3, 4, and 7).

"Student power" is a reality. Protest, vandalism, violence, and "dropping
out" are evidence that it must be dealt with in positive ways. Curricula
which confront the social issues of the day and the psychological needs
of students can help turn this "power" into a positive force (see Chapters 2 and 7).

Recommendation 5   Those in the school should make every effort to
involve a variety of people in their programs for people are the "raw
material" of education.

Schools must seriously consider various forms of differentiated staffing—
part-time personnel, artists, craftsmen, or professionals in residence,
paid paraprofessionals, and community volunteers (see Chapter 7).

In bringing people into the school program, the school should look for
more than technical skills. Characteristics such as openness, willingness
to learn, empathy, internal locus of control, concern for others, creativity, motivation, and social awareness are important qualities needed
by people who live and work in schools (see Chapters 2, 5, and 7).

Recommendation 6   Schools should develop a variety of alternative
programs which fit the variety of needs and interests of students and
their parents—schools without walls, multicultural programs, schools-
within-a-school, open classrooms (see Chapters 3 and 7).

Recommendation 7   Schools should be designed as places where people can reach self-fulfillment and where they can prepare for the
future. School programs should be directed at meeting the needs of
students who will live in the future.

Because of changing patterns of family life, schools must consciously set
about to (1) design appropriate early childhood education programs,
(2) establish a climate wherein the affective development of students
is enhanced, and (3) eliminate sex role stereotypes which presently
permeate curricula (see Chapter 2).

Because of the growing alienation of individuals in and from society,
schools should concentrate upon the development of student-problem-
solving and critical-thinking abilities (see Chapter 2).

Because schools are often unique in bringing together a varied sample
of human beings, they should concentrate on the development of
social skills. Wherever possible, the attempt should be made to move
students into the communities to practice what has been taught.
Undergirding the school's efforts should be a well-developed human

support system of nondirective counseling and guidance (see Chapters 2 and 7).

Schools at all levels should examine and pursue their potential for providing continuing education for adults in their communities. Both vocational and avocational programs should be considered (see Chapter 2).

Schools should provide students with programs which recognize that we live in an interdependent world. Literature, art, music, and history from around the world need to be studied instead of only that of the Western world or the United States. Further, there needs to be an emphasis upon the commonalities of men rather than upon their differences (see Chapter 2).

Recommendation 8 Practitioners in the schools should cease taking themselves and their work for granted and instead should be constantly asking and consistently seeking answers to questions concerning the educational enterprise.

In simplest form, these questions include: What are we attempting to do? How are we going about it? How well are we doing? How can we do better? And ultimately, "Is our school a *good* place for us and for students to live in and to learn?"

Inherent in all that has been said throughout this book is the theme that schools are in transition. What has been written here is intended to help clarify the movement and perhaps to direct its thrust. We sincerely hope that our readers have found it helpful.

APPENDIX A
GUIDELINES FOR APPLYING FOR GRANT FUNDS

It is often felt that proposal writing is relatively simple, that it takes only a good idea and a good editor. And yet, many good ideas do not get funded, some for political reasons, others because of bad timing. A major problem which can be avoided, however, is that of letting a good idea get somehow lost in fuzzy rationale or "pedagogese."

Various funding agencies require differing amounts and kinds of information when proposals are submitted for funding. Once you decide on the appropriate agency for the proposal, you should obtain guidelines from that agency, if they are available, and follow the guidelines in the preparation of the proposal.

Prior to that, however, there are some steps which can and should be taken that will both clarify your thinking and aid in writing the final proposal for submission. By following such steps, you should be able to prepare a better proposal which will receive maximum consideration.

1   *The idea.* Obviously, if you want funds, you want them for something! Start by writing your idea down in *as brief a form as possible*. One or two paragraphs should do. Don't let your idea get lost in pages of justification or rationale. This comes later.

2   *Type of proposal.* Generally, there are three reasons for applying for funds. At one level, you may wish to develop an idea. Many agencies provide planning money or "seed money" for such activities. At another level, you may wish to pilot or experiment with an idea that is already developed. Finally, you may wish to operationalize or demonstrate an idea which has been fully developed and successfully piloted or field tested. Usually, this type of proposal is quite complex and requires substantially more funding.

159

3   *Need and justification.* Show why there is a need for your idea. Give evidence that you have analyzed your target population and that your idea is related to this analysis. Review pertinent research and relate it concisely to your analysis and to your idea. Build all of this into a rationale which clearly states or explains the basic principles or assumptions which underly your objectives or hypotheses.

4   *Objectives or hypotheses.* Analyze your idea. Generally, it will have many components. Identify all components and state them as objectives. As much as possible state such objectives in behavioral terms so that they will provide guidance for evaluation. If possible, consider how you will evaluate your project. If your proposal is for research, state your hypotheses.

5   *Procedures.* Tell concisely how you plan to meet each objective. Expand your idea into a program of action, relating each phase to its appropriate objective. If your proposal is for research, lay out your research design.

6   *Evaluation.* State how you plan to evaluate the changes in behavior in your target population. State your criteria. Name the instruments you plan to use, describe the type of instrumentation you might develop, or list the quantitative measures you plan to use.

7   *Dissemination.* Describe how you plan to disseminate your findings as a result of your proposal. If possible, identify the target population(s) to which you plan to disseminate findings. If possible, relate your methods of dissemination to the characteristics of your target group(s), considering modes of decision making, influence, communication, etc.

8   *System or model.* If possible, design a system or build a model which is representative of the real world in which your idea will intervene. Any model or systems design should clearly show relationships and should aid you in making predictions.

9   *Time and phase out.* Define the length of the program you propose. If possible, indicate how proposed funding will be phased out at the end of the program and how local funding will take over if necessary.

10   *Resources.* Itemize all resources necessary to the plan including personnel, consultant help, space, equipment, material, travel, and even the telephone bill. Document the need for such resources in terms of your rationale. In the matter of personnel and consultants, list qualifications necessary for professionals, and, if possible, name the specific persons if they have tentatively agreed to serve. Do not, as some proposal writers do, list all the big names in the field in which the proposal seems to fall, hoping to impress those who review the proposal.

If these elements are written out in a concise manner (there are very few proposals which should exceed 15–20 pages), they can be worked into the format required by any specific agency.

APPENDIX B
REFERENCES FROM THE TEXT

Accountability: Review of Literature and Recommendations for Implementation, North Carolina Department of Public Instruction, Division of Planning, Research, and Development, May 1972, chap. 7.

Advisory Committee on Intergovernmental Relations: *Metropolitan Social and Economic Disparities: Implications for Intergovernmental Relations in Central Cities and Suburbs,* U.S. Government Printing Office, Washington, D.C., 1965, chap. 7.

Almond, Gabriel A.: "A Functional Approach to Comparative Politics," in Gabriel A. Almond and James S. Coleman (eds.), *The Politics of Developing Areas,* Princeton University Press, Princeton, N.J., 1960, chap. 3.

———, and G. Bingham Powell, Jr.: *Comparative Politics: A Developmental Approach,* Little, Brown, Boston, 1966, chap. 7.

Argyris, Chris: *Personality and Organization: The Conflict between System and Individual,* Harper & Row, New York, 1957, chaps. 3, 5.

Association of California School Administrators: *Project Leadership—What Can It Do?* Project Leadership, the Association, Irvine, Calif., 1970, chap. 6.

Bailey, Stephen K.: "The Office of Education and the Education Act of 1965," in Michael W. Kirst (ed.), *The Politics of Education at the Local, State and Federal Levels,* McCutchan Publishing Corporation, Berkeley, Calif., 1970, chap. 4.

———: "Teachers' Centres: A British First," *Phi Delta Kappan,* November 1971, pp. 146–149, chap. 6.

Beckhard, Richard: *Organizational Development, Strategies and Methods,* Addison-Wesley, Reading, Mass., 1969, chap. 5.

Belisle, Eugene L., and Cyril G. Sargent: "The Concept of Administration," in Roald F. Campbell and Russell T. Gregg (eds.), *Administrative Behavior in Education,* Harper & Row, New York, 1957, chap. 5.

Bellack, Arno, et al.: "Action Research in Schools," *Teachers College Record,* vol. 54, pp. 246–255, 1953, chap. 5.

163

Bengelsdorf, Irving S.: *Spaceship Earth: People and Pollution,* Fox-Mathes Publication, Los Angeles, 1969, chap. 2.

Bennis, Warren G., Kenneth D. Benne, and Robert Chin: *The Planning of Change,* 2d ed., Holt, New York, 1969, chap. 5.

Bentzen, Mary M.: "Conflicting Roles," in Jerrold M. Novotney (ed.), *The Principal and the Challenge of Change,* |I|D(E|A|, Melbourne, Fla., 1968, chap. 3.

————: "A Peer Group Strategy for Intervention in Schools," unpublished paper, Institute for Development of Educational Activities, Inc., Research Division, Los Angeles, 1970, chap. 7.

————, and Associates: *Changing Schools: The Magic Feather Principle,* McGraw-Hill, New York, 1974, chaps. 1, 7.

————, and Kenneth A. Tye: "Effecting Change in Elementary Schools," in John I. Goodlad and Harold G. Shane (eds.), *The Elementary School in the United States,* the Seventy-second Yearbook of the National Society for the Study of Education, Part II, The University of Chicago Press, Chicago, 1973, chap. 7.

Brademas, John: "The Case for Categorical Aid," in Michael W. Kirst (ed.), *The Politics of Education at the Local, State and Federal Levels,* McCutchan Publishing Corporation, Berkeley, Calif., 1970, chap. 4.

Bradford, Leland P.: "Developing Potentials through Class Groups," in Leland P. Bradford (ed.), *Human Forces in Teaching and Learning,* National Training Laboratory, National Education Association, Washington, D.C., 1961, chap. 7.

————, Jack R. Gibb, and Kenneth D. Benne: *T-Group Theory and Laboratory Method,* Wiley, New York, 1964, chap. 5.

Brameld, Theodore: *The Climactic Decades,* Praeger, New York, 1970, chap. 1.

Brown, George: *Human Teaching for Human Learning,* Viking, New York, 1971, chap. 7.

Bruner, Jerome, Jacqueline J. Goodnew, and George A. Austin: *A Study of Thinking,* Science Editions, Wiley, New York, 1967, chap. 7.

Burstall, Clare, et al.: *Primary French in the Balance,* NFER Publishing Co., Windsor, Berks, England, 1974, chap. 4.

Callahan, Raymond E.: *Education and the Cult of Efficiency,* University of Chicago Press, Chicago, 1962, chap. 7.

Campbell, Roald F., and Donald H. Layton: *Policy Making for American Education,* The University of Chicago, Midwest Administration Center, Chicago, 1969, chap. 4.

————, and Tim L. Mazzoni (eds.): *State Policy Making for the Public Schools: A Comparative Analysis,* Educational Governance Project, Ohio State University, Columbus, 1974, chap. 4.

Carlson, Richard O.: "School Superintendents and the Adoption of Modern Math: A Social Structures Profile," in Matthew B. Miles (ed.), *Innovation in Education,* Teachers College Press, Columbia University, New York, 1964, chap. 4.

————, et al.: *Change Processes in Public Schools,* The Center for the Advanced Study of Educational Administration, Eugene, Oreg., 1965, chap. 4.

Carroll, John B.: "Research on Teaching Foreign Languages," in Stanley Levenson and William Kendrick (eds.), *Readings in Foreign Languages for the Elementary School,* Blaisdell, Waltham, Mass., 1967, chap. 4.

Chesler, Mark, et al.: "Affecting Political and Structural Change in Schools," in Ronald G. Havelock and Mary Havelock, *Training for Change Agents,* Center for Research Utilization of Scientific Knowledge (CRUSK), Institute for Social Research, Ann Arbor, Mich., 1972, chap. 7.

Chin, Robert: "Models and Ideas about Changing," in W. C. Meierhenry (ed.), *Media and Educational Innovation,* University of Nebraska Press, Lincoln, 1963, chap. 5.

Clark, David, and Egon Guba: "An Examination of Potential Change Roles," paper presented at the Symposium on Innovation in Planning School Curricula, Airlee House, Va., October 1965, chap. 6.

Coleman, James S., and Others: *Youth: Transition to Adulthood,* Report of the Panel on Youth of the President's Science Advisory Committee, The University of Chicago Press, Chicago, 1974, chap. 2.

Colm, Gerhard: "Prospective Economic Development," in *Prospective Changes in Society by 1980,* Designing Education for the Future, an Eight-State Project, Denver, 1966, chap. 2.

Committee on Labor and Public Welfare, United States Senate: *Catalyst for Change: A National Study of ESEA Title III,* U.S. Government Printing Office, 1967, chap. 5.

Corey, Stephen M.: *Action Research to Improve School Practices,* Teachers College Press, Columbia University, New York, 1953, chap. 5.

Cornell, Terry D.: *Performance and Process Objectives,* Educational Innovations Press, Tucson, Ariz., 1970, chap. 7.

Cremin, Lawrence A.: *The Transformation of the School,* Vintage Books, Random House, New York, 1961, chap. 1.

Culver, Carmen M., David A. Shiman, and Ann Lieberman: "Working Together: The Peer Group Strategy," in Carmen M. Culver and Gary J. Hoban (eds.), *The Power to Change: Issues for the Innovative Educator,* McGraw-Hill, New York, 1973, chap. 7.

Delgado, Jose M.: *Physical Control of the Mind: Toward a Psycho-civilized Society,* Harper & Row, New York, 1969, chap. 2.

Dewey, John: *Democracy and Education,* Macmillan, New York, 1916, chap. 7.

Downey, Lawrence W.: "Direction Amid Change," *Phi Delta Kappan,* February 1961, chap. 5.

Easton, David: *A Framework for Political Analysis,* Prentice-Hall, Englewood Cliffs, N.J., 1965, chap. 7.

Education Summary, National School Public Relations Association, Washington, D.C., Nov. 6, 1972, chap. 7.

Eichholz, Gerhard C.: "Why Do Teachers Reject Change?" *Theory into Practice,* vol. 2, pp. 264–268, December 1963, chap. 6.

Fantini, Mario: "Alternatives within Public Schools," *Phi Delta Kappan,* vol. 54, pp. 444–448, March 1973, chap. 7.

Fayol, Henri: *General and Industrial Management,* Patman and Sons, Ltd., London, 1949, chap. 5.

Feldman, Max L.: "Transportation: An Equal Opportunity for Access," in William R. Ewald, Jr. (ed.), *Environment and Policy: The Next Fifty Years,* Indiana University Press, Bloomington, 1968, chap. 2.

Flachs, Richard: "Strategies for Radical Social Change," *Social Policy,* March–April, 1971, chap. 2.

Follett, Mary Parker: *Creative Experience,* Longmans, London, 1924, chap. 5.

Foundation Profiles, Taft Products, Inc., Washington, D.C., 1973, chap. 6.

French, John P., and Bertram H. Raven: "The Bases of Social Power," in Dorwin Cartwright (ed.), *Studies in Social Power,* Institute for Social Research, Research Center for Group Dynamics, University of Michigan, 1959, chap. 6.

Frymier, Jack R.: *Fostering Educational Change,* Merrill, Columbus, Ohio, 1969, chap. 5.

Furth, Hans G.: *Piaget and Knowledge,* Prentice-Hall, Englewood Cliffs, N.J., 1969, chap. 7.

Gardner, John: *No Easy Victories,* Harper & Row, New York, 1968, chap. 1.

―――: *Self-Renewal: The Individual and the Innovative Society,* Harper & Row, New York, 1963, chap. 7.

Gittell, Marilyn: "The Balance of Power and the Community School," in Henry M. Levin (ed.), *Community Control of Schools,* The Brookings Institution, Washington, D.C., 1970, chap. 7.

―――, and T. Edward Hollander: *Six Urban School Districts: A Comparative Study of Institutional Response,* Praeger, New York, 1968, chap. 7.

Glasser, William: *Schools without Failure,* Harper & Row, New York, 1969, chap. 7.

Goodlad, John I.: "The Individual School and Its Principal: Key Setting and Key Person," *Educational Leadership,* vol. 13, October 1956, chap. 1.

―――: "The Teacher Selects, Plans, Organizes," in *Learning and the Teacher,* Association for Supervision and Curriculum Development, Washington, D.C., 1959, chap. 4.

―――, M. Frances Klein, and Associates: *Looking Behind the Classroom Door,* rev. ed., Charles A. Jones Publishing Co., Worthington, Ohio, 1974, chap. 4.

―――, ―――, Jerrold M. Novotney, and Associates, *Early Schooling in the United States,* McGraw-Hill, New York, 1973, chap. 2.

―――, ―――, ―――, Kenneth A. Tye, and Associates, *Toward a Mankind*

School: An Adventure in Humanistic Education, McGraw-Hill, New York, 1974, chaps. 1, 2, 3, 6.

————, and Maurice N. Richter, Jr.: *The Development of a Conceptual System for Dealing with Problems of Curriculum and Instruction,* U.S. Office of Education, Cooperative Research Report, SACE 8024, Project No. 454, 1967, chap. 4.

Goodman, Paul: *Compulsory Mis-Education,* Horizon Press, New York, 1965, chap. 1.

Gordon, Theodore H.: *The Future,* Martin Press, New York, 1965, chap. 2.

Gordon, William J.: *The Metaphorical Way of Learning and Knowing,* Synectics Education Press, Cambridge, Mass., 1970, chap. 7.

Greenleaf, Warren T., and Gary A. Griffin: *Schools for the Seventies and Beyond: A Call to Action,* a staff report, Center for the Study of Instruction, National Education Association, Washington, D.C., 1971, chap. 2.

Greenstein, Fred I.: *Children and Politics,* Yale, New Haven, 1965, chap. 1.

Gross, Neal: *Who Runs Our Schools?* Wiley, New York, 1958, chap. 4.

Guba, Egon G.: "Development, Diffusion and Evaluation," in T. L. Eidell and Joanne M. Ketchel (eds.), *Knowledge, Production and Utilization in Educational Administration,* Center for Advanced Study of Educational Administration, University of Oregon, Eugene, 1968, chap. 6.

Hage, Jerald, and Michael Aiken: *Social Change in Complex Organizations,* Random House, New York, 1970, chap. 3.

Hall, Calvin S., and Gardner Lindzey: *Theories of Personality,* Wiley, New York, 1957, chap. 5.

Halpin, Andrew W., and Don B. Croft: *The Organizational Climate of Schools,* U.S. Office of Education, Washington, D.C., 1962, chap. 3.

Harman, Willis W.: *The Nature of Our Changing Society: Implications for Schools,* ERIC Clearinghouse on Educational Administration, Eugene, Oreg., 1969, chaps. 5, 7.

Harris, Raymond P.: *American Education: Facts, Fancies and Folklore,* Random House, New York, 1961, chap. 1.

Havelock, Ronald G.: *Guide to Innovation in Education,* Center for Research on Utilization of Scientific Knowledge (CRUSK), Institute for Social Research, University of Michigan, Ann Arbor, 1970. Also issued as *The Change Agent's Guide to Innovation in Education,* Educational Technology Publications, Inc., Englewood Cliffs, N.J., 1973, chap. 6.

————: *Planning for Innovation through Dissemination and Utilization of Knowledge,* Center for Research on Utilization of Scientific Knowledge (CRUSK), Institute for Social Research, University of Michigan, Ann Arbor, 1971, chap. 4.

Havighurst, Robert J. (ed.): *Metropolitanism: Its Challenges to Education,* the Sixty-seventh Yearbook of the National Society for the Study of Education, Part I, The University of Chicago Press, Chicago, 1968, chap. 7.

Hawley, Ann (ed.): *Contact Washington,* Washington Internships in Education, Washington, D.C., 1969, chap. 4.

Hentoff, Nat: *Our Children Are Dying,* Viking, New York, 1965, chap. 1.

Hess, Robert D., and Judith V. Torney: *The Development of Political Attitudes in Children,* Aldine, Chicago, 1967, chap. 1.

Holmes, Emory J.: "Community Representation in Educational Decision Making: An Exploratory Case Study of School-Community Advisory Councils," unpublished doctoral dissertation, University of California, Los Angeles, 1972, chap. 7.

Holt, John: *How Children Fail,* Dell Publishing Co., New York, 1965, chap. 1.

————: *How Children Learn,* Pitman, New York, 1967, chap. 7.

Homitz, Wallace I.: "A Study of Demand upon the School Boards in a Unified and an Independent Junior College District," unpublished doctoral dissertation, University of California, Los Angeles, 1967, chap. 7.

Howe, Harold H.: "Respect, Engagement, Responsibility," in *The Struggle for Power in the Public Schools,* National Committee for the Support of the Public Schools, Sixth Annual Conference Report, Washington, D.C., March 17–19, 1968, chap. 4.

Ianaccone, Lawrence: "An Approach to the Informal Organization of the School," in Daniel E. Griffiths (ed.), *Behavioral Science and Educational Administration,* the Sixty-third Yearbook of the National Society for the Study of Education, Part II, The University of Chicago Press, Chicago, 1964, chap. 3.

|I|D|E|A|: "The Chemical Transfer of Memory: Research and Implications," an |I|D|E|A| Occasional Paper, Information and Service Division, P. O. Box 446, Melbourne, Fla. 32901, 1970, chap. 2.

|I|D|E|A|: *The Problem Solving School Program Kit,* Institute for Development of Educational Activities, Inc., Information and Services Division, P. O. Box 446, Melbourne, Fla. 32901, chap. 6.

Illich, Ivan D.: *Celebration of Awareness: A Call for Institutional Revolution,* Doubleday, Garden City, N.Y., 1970, chaps. 1, 7.

Janowitz, Morris: *Institution Building in Urban Education,* Russell Sage Foundation, Connecticut Printers, Inc., Hartford, 1969, chap. 6.

Joyce, Bruce, and Marsha Weil: *Models of Teaching,* Prentice-Hall, Englewood Cliffs, N.J., 1972, chap. 7.

Jung, Charles C.: "The Trainer Change Agent Role within a School System," in Goodwin Watson (ed.), *Change in School Systems,* National Training Laboratory, Institute for Applied Behavioral Science, National Education Association, Washington, D.C., 1967, chaps. 5, 6.

————, et al.: *Interpersonal Communication,* Xerox, Inc., Sterling Forest, N.Y., 1972, chap. 3.

Kahn, Herman, and Anthony J. Weiner: *The Year 2000: A Framework for Speculation on the Next Thirty-three Years,* Macmillan, New York, 1967, chap. 2.

Knox, Owen: "Processing Environmental Demands: A Case Study for Decentralization," unpublished doctoral dissertation, University of California, Los Angeles, 1971, chap. 7.

Kohl, Herbert R.: *The Open Classroom: A Practical Guide to a New Way of Teaching*, Vintage Books, New York, 1969, chap. 7.

Leonard, George: *Education and Ecstasy*, Delacorte Press, New York, 1968, chaps. 1, 7.

Lessinger, Leon M.: *Every Kid a Winner: Accountability in Education*, Simon & Schuster, New York, 1970, chap. 7.

Lewin, Kurt: "Group Decision and Social Change," in Guy E. Swanson et al. (eds.), *Readings in Social Psychology*, Henry Holt and Company, Inc., New York, 1952, chap. 6.

Lipham, James M.: "Leadership and Administration," in *Behavioral Science and Educational Administration*, the Sixty-third Yearbook of the National Society for the Study of Education, Part II, University of Chicago Press, Chicago, 1964, chap. 5.

Lippitt, Ronald, Jeanne Watson, and Bruce Wesley: *The Dynamics of Planned Change*, Harcourt, Brace, New York, 1958, chap. 5.

Louis Harris and Associates, Inc.: "The *Life* Poll: Crisis in the High Schools," *Life Magazine*, vol. 56, no. 19, May 16, 1969, chap. 6.

McGregor, Douglas: *The Human Side of Enterprise*, McGraw-Hill, New York, 1960, chaps. 5, 6.

Marland, Sidney P.: "A New Order for Educational Research and Development," *Phi Delta Kappan*, vol. 52, no. 10, pp. 576–579, June 1971, chap. 4.

Marrow, Alfred: *The Practical Theorist: The Life and Work of Kurt Lewin*, Basic Books, New York, 1969, chap. 5.

Maslow, Abraham: "A Theory of Human Motivation," *Psychological Review*, vol. 50, pp. 370–396, 1943, chaps. 3, 5.

Massialas, Byron, and Benjamin Cox: *Inquiry in Social Studies*, McGraw-Hill, New York, 1966, chap. 7.

Mayer, Morton: *The Schools*, Harper & Row, New York, 1961, chap. 1.

Mayo, Elton: *The Human Problems of an Industrial Civilization*, Boston Graduate School of Business Administration, Harvard University, Cambridge, Mass., 1946, chap. 5.

Michael, Donald R.: "Factors Inhibiting and Facilitating the Acceptance of Educational Innovations," Institute of Government and Public Affairs, University of California, Los Angeles, 1964, chap. 5.

———: *The Unprepared Society: Planning for a Precarious Future*, Basic Books, New York, 1968, chap. 5.

Miles, Matthew B.: "Planned Change and Organizational Health: Figure and Ground," in Richard O. Carlson (ed.), *Change Processes in the Public Schools*, CASEA, University of Oregon, Eugene, 1969, chap. 5.

——— (ed.): *Innovation in Education*, Teachers College, Columbia University Press, New York, 1964, chap. 5.

————, and Dale Lake: "Self-Renewal in School Systems: A Strategy for Planned Change," in Goodwin Watson (ed.), *Concepts for Social Change,* National Training Laboratory, Institute for Applied Behavioral Sciences, Washington, D.C., 1967, chaps. 6, 7.

Mitchell, William C.: *Sociological Analysis and Politics: The Theories of Talcott Parsons,* Prentice-Hall, Englewood Cliffs, N.J., 1967, chap. 7.

National Education Association, Research Division: "High Spots in State Legislation," the Association, report published yearly, chap. 4.

National Education Association, Research Division: *Rankings of the States, 1971,* Washington, D.C., 1971, chap. 4.

Newlin, Bruce C.: "Proportional Representation and the Winton Act: A Functional-Systems Analysis," unpublished doctoral dissertation, University of California, Los Angeles, 1971, chap. 7.

Novotney, Jerrold M.: "T-Groups and Team Teaching," *The California Journal for Instructional Improvement,* vol. 10, pp. 242–247, December 1967, chap. 5.

Nystrand, Raphael O., and Luvern L. Cunningham: "Federated Urban School Systems: Compromising the Centralization-Decentralization Issue," in Frank W. Lutz (ed.), *Toward Improved Urban Education,* Charles A. Jones, Worthington, Ohio, 1970, chap. 7.

Oliver, Donald W., and James P. Shaver: *Teaching Public Issues in the High School,* Houghton-Mifflin, Boston, 1966, chap. 7.

Parker, Don H.: *Schooling for What?* McGraw-Hill, New York, 1970, chap. 2.

Pentz, Walter: "The Effect of Population Changes upon the Demands Made by the Public and Junior College Trustees," unpublished doctoral dissertation, University of California, Los Angeles, 1967, chap. 7.

"Performance Contracting," |I'D|E|A| *Reporter,* Institute for Development of Educational Activities, Inc., Information and Services Division, Melbourne, Fla., Winter 1970, chap. 7.

Postman, Neil, and Charles Weingarten: *Teaching as a Subversive Activity,* Dell, New York, 1969, chap. 1.

Quie, Albert H.: "The Case for General Aid," in Michael W. Kirst (ed.), *The Politics of Education at the Local, State, and Federal Levels,* McCutchan Publishing Corporation, Berkeley, Calif., 1970, chap. 4.

Rand, M. John, and Fenwick English: "Towards a Differentiated Teaching Staff," *Phi Delta Kappan,* vol. 49, pp. 264–268, January 1968, chap. 7.

Raywid, Mary Anne: *The Ax-Grinders,* Macmillan, New York, 1962, chaps. 3, 7.

Rogers, Carl R.: *Freedom to Learn,* Merrill, Columbus, Ohio, 1969, chap. 7.

————: "A Practical Plan for Educational Revolution," in Richard R. Goulet (ed.), *Educational Change: The Reality and the Promise,* Citation Press, New York, 1968, chap. 5.

Rogers, Everett M.: *Diffusion of Innovations,* Free Press, New York, 1969, chap. 6.

Rubin, Louis J.: *Facts and Feelings in the Classroom,* Walker and Co., New York, 1973, chap. 5.

Rusch, Charles: "MOBOC: A Mobile Learning Environment," in Gary Coates (ed.), *Alternative Learning Environments*, Dowden, Hutchinson, Ross, Inc., Stroudsburg, Pa., 1974, chap. 2.

Sand, Ole: "Strategies for Change," in *The Curriculum: Retrospect and Prospect*, the Seventieth Yearbook of the National Society for the Study of Education, Part I, The University of Chicago Press, Chicago, 1971, chap. 7.

Sarason, Seymour B.: *The Culture of the School and the Problem of Change*, Allyn and Bacon, Boston, 1971, chap. 5.

Schmuck, Richard, Phillip J. Runkel, and Daniel Langmeyer: "Improving Organizational Problem Solving in a School Faculty," *Applied Behavioral Science*, vol. 5, no. 4, October/November/December 1969, chap. 6.

Schrag, Peter: "Boston: Education's Last Hurrah," *Saturday Review*, May 21, 1966, pp. 56–58, chap. 7.

Schutz, William: *Joy: Expanding Human Awareness*, Grove Press, N.Y., 1967, chap. 7.

Schwab, Joseph J., Supervisor, Biological Sciences Curriculum Study: *Biology Teachers Handbook*, Wiley, New York, 1965, chap. 7.

Seeman, Alice Z., and Melvin Seeman: "Staff Processes and Pupil Attitudes: A Study of Teacher Participation in Educational Change," unpublished paper, chap. 2.

Selden, David: "Productivity, Yes. Accountability, No," *Nation's Schools*, vol. 89, May 1972, chap. 7.

Silberman, Charles: *Crisis in the Classroom: The Remaking of American Education*, Random House, New York, 1970, chaps. 1, 4.

————: "Murder in the Schoolroom," *Atlantic Monthly*, vol. 225, no. 6, June 1970, chap. 1.

Skinner, B. F.: *Beyond Freedom and Dignity*, Knopf, New York, 1971, chap. 7.

Smith, Vernon H.: "Options in Public Education: The Quiet Revolution," *Phi Delta Kappan*, vol. 54, pp. 434–435, March 1973, chap. 7.

Suchman, J. Richard: *Inquiry Development Program: Developing Inquiry*, Science Research Associates, Chicago, 1966, chap. 7.

Sullivan, M. W.: *Programmed English: A Modern Grammar for High School and College Students*, Macmillan, New York, 1963, chap. 7.

Taba, Hilda: *Teacher's Handbook for Elementary Social Studies*, Addison-Wesley, Reading, Mass., 1967, chap. 7.

Taber, Julian, Robert Glaser, and H. Schaeffer Halmuth: *Learning and Programmed Instruction*, Addison-Wesley, Reading, Mass., 1965, chap. 7.

Taylor, Frederick W.: *Scientific Management*, Harper & Row, New York, 1947, chap. 5.

Thelen, Herbert: *Education and the Human Quest*, Harper & Row, New York, 1960, chap. 7.

Thut, I. N.: *The Story of Education: Philosophical and Historical Foundations*, McGraw-Hill, New York, 1957, chap. 1.

Toffler, Alvin: *Future Shock,* Random House, New York, 1970, chap. 2.

Tye, Kenneth A.: "A Conceptual Framework for Political Analysis, Public Demands and School Board Decisions," unpublished doctoral dissertation, University of California, Los Angeles, 1968, chaps. 3, 4, 5, 7.

————: "Creating Disequilibrium," in *The Principal and the Challenge of Change,* |I|D|E|A| Monograph, Institute for Development of Educational Activities, Inc., Melbourne, Fla., 1968, chap. 5.

————: "Creating Impact," Division of Plans and Supplementary Centers, Bureau of Elementary and Secondary Education, U.S. Office of Education, Washington, D.C., 1967 (mimeo), chap. 6.

————: "The Political Linkage Agent," in Ronald G. Havelock and Mary Havelock, *Training for Change Agents,* Center for Research Utilization of Scientific Knowledge (CRUSK), Institute for Social Research, Ann Arbor, Mich., 1972, chap. 7.

————: "The Process," unpublished case study, Research Division, |I|D|E|A|, Los Angeles, 1972, chap. 4.

Tyler, Louise L., M. Frances Klein, and William B. Michael: *Recommendations for Curriculum and Instructional Materials,* Tyl Press, Los Angeles, 1971; rev. ed., Educational Resource Associates, Los Angeles, 1975, chap. 6.

Tyler, Ralph: "Purpose, Scope and Organization of Education," in *Implications for Education of Prospective Changes in Society,* Designing Education for the Future, an Eight-State Project, Denver, 1967, chap. 2.

U.S. Commission on Instructional Technology, *To Improve Learning,* Committee on Education and Labor, House of Representatives, Washington, D.C., March 1970, chap. 6.

U.S. Office of Management and Budget: *Catalog of Federal Domestic Assistance,* U.S. Government Printing Office, Washington, D.C., updated annually, chap. 6.

Watson, Bernard C.: "Rebuilding the System: Practical Goal or Impossible Dream?" *Phi Delta Kappan,* vol. 52, pp. 349–363, February 1971, chap. 7.

Watson, Goodwin: "Resistance to Change," in Goodwin Watson (ed.), *Concepts for Social Change,* National Training Laboratory, Institute for Applied Behavioral Science, National Education Association, Washington, D.C., 1967, chap. 5.

————: "Toward a Conceptual Architecture of a Self-Renewing School System," in Goodwin Watson (ed.), *Change in School Systems,* National Training Laboratory, Institute for Applied Behavioral Science, National Education Association, Washington, D.C., 1967, chap. 5.

White House Conference on Children, Report from Forum 5: "Learning Toward A.D. 2000," December 13–18, 1970, chap. 2.

Williams, Richard C.: "A Plan for an Accountable Elementary School District," in Carmen M. Culver and Gary J. Hoban (eds.), *The Power to Change: Issues for the Innovative Educator,* McGraw-Hill, New York, 1973, chap. 7.

————, Charles C. Wall, W. Michael Martin, and Arthur Berchin: *Effecting Organizational Renewal in Schools: A Social Systems Perspective,* McGraw-Hill, New York, 1974, chap. 3.

INDEX